HAMEL'S JOURNAL
and a description of the
KINGDOM OF KOREA
1653 – 1666

by
HENDRIK HAMEL

Translated from the original Dutch manuscript
by
Jean-Paul Buys

3rd Revised Edition

2011
The Royal Asiatic Society
Korea Branch • Seoul

Published for the Royal Asiatic Society
Korea Branch
by Seoul Press

Printed in Seoul, Korea

ISBN 89-7225-086-4   93910

My gratitude to those who encouraged me, helped me, did research, corrected me — Horace, Fred, Johannes, John, Anthony, Tienke, James and Beverly.

MAP OF KOREA

SHOWING ROUTES FOLLOWED

BY THE DUTCH SAILORS

't Oprechte JOURNAEL,

Van de ongeluckige Reyse van 't Jacht de 562D27

SPERWER,

Varende van Batavia na Tyowan en Fermosa / in 't Jaer 1653. en van daer na Japan / daer Schipper op was Reynier Egbertsz. van Amsterdam.

Beschrijvende hoe het Jacht door storm en onweer op Quelpaerts Eylant vergaen is / op hebbende 64. Man / daer van 36. aen Lant zijn geraeckt / en gevangen genomen van den Gouverneur van 't Eplant / die haer als Slaven na den Coninck van Corre dede voeren / alwaer sy 13. Jaren en 28. dagen hebben in Slavernij moeten blijven / waren in die tijdt tot op 16. nae gestorven : Daer van acht persoonen in 't Jaer 1666. met een kleyn Barckupgh zijn 't ontkomen / achterlatende noch acht van haer Maets En hoe sy in 't Vaderlandt zijn aengekomen Anno 1668. in de Maent Julp.

t'AMSTERDAM, Gedruckt

Bp GILLIS JOOSTEN SAAGMAN, in de Nieuwe-straet / Ordinaris Drucker van de Zee-Journalen en Landt-Reysen.

14

Frontispiece of the Saagman edition, Amsterdam, 1669

Bethoort by: Werken uitgegeven door de Linschoten-Vereeniging. Deel XVIII

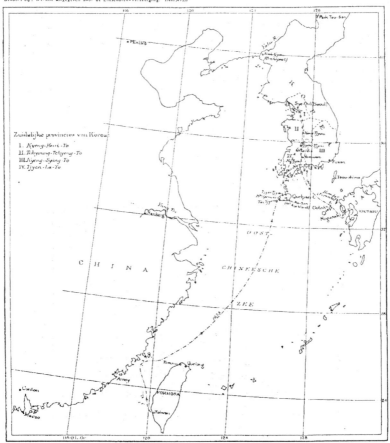

Tochten van Hendrik Hamel in 1653, 1654 en 1666.

Lith. J. Smnlders & Co., Den Haag.

TABLE OF CONTENTS

* * *

Master Eibokken on the Korean Language:

INTRODUCTION

Hendrik Hamel's account of his unexpected and involuntary visit to Korea from 1653 to 1666 has long been known as the earliest report in a western language on the land, people and customs of Korea, yet for over 300 years the only version available in English has been the very flawed Churchill translation of an embroidered French version of the text.

Gari Ledyard in his work *The Dutch Come to Korea*, shows up the errors in the Churchill translation and sheds new light on the account, but unfortunately he did not provide a new English version of Hamel's text.

That gap has now been filled and for the first time we have a direct translation into English of the original Dutch document. Jean-Paul Buys, who is himself Dutch and has lived in Japan and Korea for seven years each, has gone back to the definitive Dutch edition of the Middle Dutch document and prepared this excellent translation. As part of his research he has himself travelled to all of the places mentioned in the account and from his personal knowledge of Korea and of the places he has been able to understand some aspects of Hamel's descriptions that otherwise would have remained obscure.

Not only is this an interesting description of a long-gone Korea, the appended vocabulary list also provides valuable clues as to changes in the language over 300 years. Jean-Paul Buys has transcribed the Middle Dutch romanization into modern English spelling. Even granting some mis-romanization by Hamel – though it should be remembered that he lived in Korea for 13 years – one gets valuable clues as to 17th-century Korean pronunciation. An interesting case in point is the fortress of Pyŏngyŏng, which Hamel rendered as "Peingyeng". The translator has discovered that local residents to this day in fact still pronounce it as Hamel romanized it.

Jean-Paul Buys is to be congratulated on an excellent translation with informative notes in what will undoubtedly be the authoritative version from now on.

March 1994, Seoul

Horace G. Underwood

INTRODUCTION TO THE REVISED EDITION

Shortly after publication of *Hamel's Journal* a very important article by Dr. Frits Vos, Professor of the Japanese and Korean languages at the University of Leyden "Master Eibokken on Korea and the Korean Language: Supplementary Remarks to Hamel's Narrative" was brought to my attention. This study was published in the Transactions of the Royal Asiatic Society, Korea Branch, Volume L, 1975. I was quite distressed that I had not been aware of this publication. Dr. Vos writes, "Eibokken's information contains several valuable additions to Hamel's Description of the Kingdom of Corea. *His most important contribution to Witsen's work, however, is his vocabulary of 143 Korean words*". Dr. Vos gives splendid additional comentary and observations. He is the only person who could — from the old Dutch transcription of Korean words — give corrections, translations of words belonging to Middle Korean, usage in Chŏlla dialect, etc. It is certainly a privilege that we can reproduce his study as a supplement to this new edition of *Hamel's Journal*.

Moreover a number of misprints had to be corrected, also the use of *kilometers* turned out to be an anachronism. There are several possibilities of calculating the distance Hamel meant by the word '*mijl*'; maybe he meant the so-called German mile, which seamen used, about 7.4 km long. To use '*mijl*' might avoid confusion even though it is an unfamiliar word.

The renewed interest in Hamel resulted in a Korean translation by the late Prof. Kim Tae-Jin, who for years had shown his interest in the sojourn of the Dutch sailors in Chŏlla Province in the seventeenth century. A television documentary was made by KBS. In Hamel's hometown Gorinchem the location of the house, in which he was born, as well as the date of his baptism (20 August 1630), were discoverd in the archives, and last but not least a sister relationship was established with the county of Kangjin, the place of excile of Hendrik Hamel and his companions.

Seoul, Spring 1998

Jean-Paul Buys

TRANSLATOR'S PREFACE

On a Sunday morning in Kangjin, that quiet small town on the far south coast of Chŏllado, I met the parish priest, Father O'Leary, an Irish missionary. As we talked about Kangjin and the famous scholar Tasan, Chŏng Yak-young, who lived there in exile for many years in his mother's ancestral home, he said: "But you are Dutch, do you know that not far from here in the seventeenth century the Dutch who were shipwrecked on Chejudo lived in exile?" Of course I had read the study by Gari Ledyard, but I had never associated their stay in Chŏllado with any particular location.

In the efficient Korean way, a visit soon was organized and some time later two young men drove me beyond the mountain range that separates the coastal plains of Kangjin from the hinterland. I was wondering what we were going to see and I suggested maybe we should go to the village tree? "No, we are going to the primary school!" was their decided answer. We entered Pyŏngyŏng as the town is called. The main street was like the main street in any ordinary Korean country town. Then we turned into the school compound and I saw a vast space surrounded by the remains of an old fortress wall.

An informational plaque, in English, reads: SITE OF CHŎLLA MILITARY FORTRESS (Chŏllanom-do Monument No. 140) The walled military fortress was the headquarters of the Chŏlla Army during the Chosŏn Kingdom period (1382-1910)...

The Chŏlla Army Headquarters was moved here in 1417 or the 17th year of the reign of King T'aejong. It was closed down in 1895. The wall that encircled the camp is heavily damaged. But, there are many historical parts which remain to date in their original shape...

Both outer and inner parts of the wall are made with stacked rocks. In some parts where dwellings were, inside rocks are stacked only on the outer face, with the inner inside done with mud. Rocks used are mostly untreated ones and bigger rocks are placed on the bottom. There were about ten structures inside the wall including a guest house. But no traces of them can be seen today.

It was at this fortress that 33 shipwrecked Dutchmen, including Hendrik Hamel, stayed for seven years, beginning 1656 after they were rescued near Chejudo. Hamel and seven other Dutch sailors escaped from Yŏsu in 1666 and returned to the Netherlands.

Hamel's book about his shipwreck and subsequent life in Korea was the first publication ever to introduce Korea to the Western world. This incident symbolizes the beginning of the Korea Netherlands relation. (new text, shortened)

So this playground was the same square that Hamel had written about, which they had had to keep clean and to weed. As we slowly walked about, the narrative began to take on a new dimension for me. We crossed the main street and entered the village. A very large gingko tree stood next to a community house, again with a notice: "This tree is 600 years old!" Hamel and his men must have rested in the shade of that very tree. We continued towards the hills that enclose Pyŏngyŏng to the east, and reached a small river. There are some small bridges across it, and well-kept narrow streets ran alongside the water, like the banks of a canal. My imagination took over: was this not like a town in Holland, built along a canal? There was something familiar about this obviously domesticated stream. Could not our Dutchmen have helped to shape this irrigation system? Traditional towns in Holland are all built along a canal or river. Water engineering is something innate to every Hollander. These men had lived here for seven years, a long time for those who were used to working with their hands.

Back in Seoul I returned to the Hamel text and now I became all the more impatient to see the original text, the Urtext, as the existing English one is based on a French translation. The Counsellor at the Royal Netherlands Embassy, Mr. Johannes Huber, suggested we should write to the National Archives and ask for a copy of the *Hoetink* edition of Hamel's text, which had been printed from the original manuscript, about which Ledyard wrote: "This is the definitive edition, rich in commentary and supporting material", and then adds: "I was rather surprised to find that this very valuable book — consisting of a long and detailed introduction and many documentary appendices, in addition to the *previously unpublished text of the manuscript version of Hamel's account* — has been virtually unmentioned and certainly unused by any Western author writing in English" (Ledyard, 13). To which one must add that the assumed Western author would have to be able to read old Dutch and have some knowledge of Korea.

With the aid of a Middle-Dutch dictionary I set about making the first translation of this text into English, a sometimes tedious effort, but very enriching. It forced me into a form of empathy. I was more than just translating an old document. I had to try to enter into the mind of someone looking at Korean life in the seventeenth century. At a documentary exhibition about Rembrandt in Seoul, I happened to be looking at a fine etching of a landscape with a farmhouse, covered with an old thatched roof. There was a date: 1648. This was not only a splendid Rembrandt etching; this was an image of Holland as Hamel knew it. Hamel had written about Korea more than 300 years ago and he had done so as someone who had lived in Western society 300 years ago. He was examining Korean life and concepts from his own cultural perspectives.

The language of Hamel strikes one as very sober, even reticent. He seldom uses the adverb "very", therefore when he does use it, as in writing about Buddhist monasteries in the mountains "very beautifully situated in the mountains amidst woods" one feels he was impressed and rightly so. Sometimes one can sense distress, fear and loneliness in his words, and thankfulness and trust as well.

What fascinates me most though is the total solitude of the Dutch sailors. They hardly knew in which country they were, although the existence of Korea was known. Since the early part of the 16th century, Portuguese ships had visited the seas around Japan. In the records of 31 August 1643 of the VOC (The Dutch India Company, established in 1602) was written: "Our trade [with Japan] is still very young compared to the Portuguese who have frequented Japan for 100 years." Portuguese sailors and missionaries were the first to introduce Korea to the Western world. A well known Dutch navigator, Jan Huyghen van Linschoten, who sailed with the Portuguese, wrote in 1595: "The Japanese carry on trade with the people of the region called 'Cooray,' about which I have good, detailed and true information, as well as the navigation to that country.... The Portuguese call these islands 'Ilhas de Core,' meaning the islands of Korea. The largest island is called 'Chausien'.... From there towards the Goto Islands, one of the islands of Japan, is about 125 miles S.E." (*Reys-Gheschrift van de Navigatien der Portugaloysers in Orienten enz*, 1595, 70)

Being forced to stay in Korea, they must have felt that in the long run they had become a nuisance. They remained complete strangers, living in a closed society not at all used to seeing foreigners. And back home in Holland, even family members must have given up hope of ever seeing their husbands and sons again. Shipwrecks occurred, sailors were lost, people died and life had to go on. This was the case for young Mrs. Weltevree. Jan Janse had left De Rijp before his first child was born. Later, she remarried while her first son kept alive the family name of Weltevree in Holland. If Hamel had not told about Jan Janse and his life at the court in Seoul, nobody would ever have known who the man behind the Korean name Pak Yon was. Thirteen generations later, a Mr. Weltevree from Holland was present in Seoul for the dedication of a Weltevree statue in the city's Children's Park.

Last autumn I returned to Chŏlla Province with a young American scholar of Korean history. This time we took the local bus from Kangjin. The farmers were curious to know where we were going. "To Pyŏngyŏng," we answered. "Ah, Peing-yeng," confirmed a farmer's wife. Was that not how Hamel wrote it? The local dialect had not changed in all those years.

I hope this new edition of *Hamel's Journal* will help many people look anew at the first meeting of Westerners with Korea.

An old map of Chŏlla Pyŏngyŏng fortress.

HAMEL'S JOURNAL

Journal of what happened to the surviving officers and sailors of the ship Sperwer (Sparrow Hawk) from the time this ship was lost on 16 August 1653 on the island Quelpaert (belonging to the King of Korea) until 14 September 1666, when eight of the crew escaped to Nagasaki in Japan, and what happened in the Kingdom of Korea, as well as the manners of this nation and about the country.

After receiving instructions from His Excellency the Governor General and from the members of the Council of the Indies to proceed to the port of Taiwan, we left Batavia on 18 June 1653, on board of above mentioned yacht. His Excellency, Mr. Cornelis Caeser, was with us on board. He was to take over the government of Taiwan, Formosa and dependencies, replacing His Excellency, Mr. Nicolaes Verburgh, the acting governor there.

After a good and successful voyage we arrived on 16 July on the Roads of Taiwan. His Excellency went ashore and we unloaded the cargo. Then the governor and the council of Taiwan dispatched us to Japan. After having loaded our cargo and taken leave of His Excellency we set sail on 30 July from the Roads hoping for a voyage as speedy as possible in the name of God.

The last day of July the weather was fine. Towards evening a storm approached us, coming from Formosa, increasing in intensity all through the night.

On the first of August, at the dawning of the day, we found ourselves close to a small island. We did our best to cast anchor behind that island, to shelter from the strong wind and deep waves. Finally, in great danger the while, we were able to drop anchor behind the island. We were trapped there, however, since behind us was a big reef with heavy waves breaking over it. By chance, the skipper, looking out of the window of the gallery on the stern of the ship, became aware of this. If he had not, we would have been smashed on the reef and lost our ship, since the reef could not be seen in the rain and the darkness though we were only a musket shot away from it. When the day was clearing up we found ourselves so close to the Chinese coast that we could see Chinese troops busy preparing along the shore, hoping that we might run aground. But with the help of the Most High this did not happen. As the storm did not diminish but increased, we remained at anchor during that day as well as during the following night.

The morning of 2 August was very still. The Chinese were still out in force, appearing to us to be waiting like hungry wolves to catch us. In order to avoid all perils of anchors, cables and the like, we decided to lift anchor and set sail to get out of their sight and away from the coast. That day and the following night all was silent.

On the morning of 3 August, we observed that the stream had carried us away about 20 mijl. We saw the coast of Formosa again. We set our course in between (that is between the coast of Formosa and that of China). The weather was good, a little cool.

From 4 August till 11 August we often were becalmed, or had capricious winds. We drifted between the coast of China and Formosa.

On 11 August the weather turned bad again, with rain coming from the S.E. We were heading N.E. by E.N.E..

On 12, 13 and 14 August the weather grew worse and worse, with shifting winds, so that sometimes we hoisted our sails and other times used no sails at all. The sea became very boisterous. With violent lurching the ship took on a lot of water. Because of the continuing rains we had not been able to make any observations. We were forced to let the ship drift without any sail in order to avoid being tossed upon some coast.

On 15 August the wind was so strong that on deck we were unable to hear or understand one another speak, nor could we use the smallest sail. We took on so much water, that we had more than enough to do, pumping to keep the lower hold dry. Because of the tempestuous sea we sometimes took on so much water that we thought we would sink.

Towards evening the sea almost broke off the bow and the stern. The sea had loosened the bowsprit so much that we were in great peril of losing the whole bow. We used every means to secure the bow, but we did not succeed because of the terrible lurching and the high seas sweeping over us, one after the other. Seeing no better means, in order to escape the sea somewhat we thought it fit to save our lives, the ship and the company goods by loosening the foresail somewhat, by which we hoped to escape the worst the heavy storm could do (thinking that next to God, this would be the best means). While loosening the foresail a wave came over the stern, so that those working there were nearly washed away from the deck. The ship was brimful of water, whereupon the skipper shouted: "Mates, commend yourselves to God. One or two more waves like that and we must all die together. We can no longer withstand this."

About one o'clock at night, the man who was on look-out called: "Land, land!" We were but a musket shot away from it. Because of the darkness and heavy rains we had not been able to see it earlier, or become aware of it. Immediately we dropped the anchors and turned the ship about by putting over the helm. But because of the depth and the roughness of the sea and the strong wind the anchors did not hold. Then suddenly the ship hit the rocks. With three shocks, the whole ship instantly broke apart in splinters. Some of those who were down in their bunks had no time to come up to the deck to save their lives, and they paid the ultimate price. Some of those who were on deck jumped overboard, others were hurled here and there by the sea.

Fifteen of us reached land, mostly naked and quite hurt, and we thought that no others had been able to save their lives. Sitting on the rocks we still heard some moaning of men in the wreck, but because of the darkness we could not recognize anyone, nor help them.

On 16 August at the dawning of the day those who were still able to walk went along the beach, searching and calling to see whether anyone else had reached land. Here and there some others appeared and we were finally 36 altogether, most badly hurt. In the wreck we discovered a man trapped between two big barrels. Immediately we freed him. Three hours later he died. His body had been badly crushed.

We looked at one another with sadness; such a beautiful ship broken into pieces. Of the 64 men we were but 36 alive. It all had happened within a quarter of an hour. We searched for the bodies of the dead who had been washed ashore. We found the skipper, Reijnier Egbertse, from Amsterdam, about 10 to 12 fathoms (about 20 m) from the water, lying dead with one arm under his head. We immediately buried him as well as 6 or 7 sailors found dead here and there.

We also searched for any provisions that might have been washed ashore as during the last 2 or 3 days we had eaten very little; the cook had not been able to cook because of the bad weather. We found but one bag of flour, a barrel of meat, a barrel with some bacon and a small cask of red Spanish wine, which was useful for the injured people. We were most in want of fire. Since we did not see or hear anybody, we thought that the island was uninhabited. Towards noon the rain and wind abated somewhat. We were able to make a tent with pieces of the sails so that we could shelter together from the rain.

On 17 August, all of us feeling sad and forlorn, we were on the look-out for people, hoping they might be Japanese, so that with their help we might return to our country, since otherwise there seemed to be no solution, our ship and lifeboat being broken in pieces and beyond repair.

Just before noon we spotted a man, about a cannon shot away. We beckoned to him, but as soon as he saw us he ran away. Shortly after noon three men arrived only a musket shot away from the tent, but they would not approach us, whatever gestures we tried. Finally one of our men dared to go up to them. Presenting his gun, he finally succeeded in getting some fire, of which we were really in want. These men were dressed in the Chinese fashion, but they wore hats made of horsehair. We were all very afraid that we might have come to a place of pirates, or exiled Chinese. Towards evening about 100 armed men arrived near the tent. They counted our number and all through the night kept watch over us around the tent.

On the morning of the 18th we were busy making a large tent, when towards noon about 1000 or 2000 men arrived, horsemen as well as soldiers. They encamped around the tent. Assembled in ranks, they sent for the secretary (book-keeper), the chief navigation officer, the second boatswain and a ship's boy. When the four approached, the commander put around each one's neck an iron chain on which a bell was hanging (like the one the sheep in Holland have around their necks). Crawling forward, they were thrown face down in front of the commander, accompanied by such an outcry of the soldiers that it was terrible to hear. Our men in the tent, hearing and seeing what was happening, said to one another: "Our officers precede us, soon we will follow." We had been lying flat for only a moment when they gestured us to kneel. The commander asked something, but we did not understand him. We gestured and tried to indicate that we wanted to go to Nagasaki in Japan. But it was no use; we could not understand one another. They did not know the word Japan, since they call it *Oenara*, or *Ilbon*. The commander ordered each of us to be served a small cup of arrack and be brought back to the tent. Our escorts came right into the tent to see if we had any provisions, but they did not find anything except the aforementioned meat and bacon, which they showed the commander. About an hour later they brought a little boiled rice for all of us, since they thought we must be starving and too much food would hurt us.

In the afternoon they all returned, each one carrying a rope, which frightened us very much, thinking they had come to bind and kill us. But they walked towards the wreck, making a lot of commotion, and they collected everything on land that still was of use. In the evening they gave us rice to eat. That afternoon the chief navigator had made an observation and found that we were on the island of Quelpaert, at 33 degrees and 32 minutes North.[1]

On the 19th they were busy bringing goods ashore and drying them, burning any wood that contained iron. Our officers went to visit the commander and the admiral of the island, who had joined them and gave each one a pair of fieldglasses. They took with them a jar of red wine, as well as a silver cup belonging to the Company, which we had found lodged between some rocks, to pour the wine into. Tasting the wine, they liked it very much and they drank so much that they rejoiced greatly. Then they sent us back to the tent, after having shown us much friendship and giving us back the silver cup.

On the 20th they burned the wreck and all the remaining wood, in order to recover the iron. During the burning of the wreck, two charges of explosives went off, sending everyone fleeing, officers and soldiers. Returning shortly afterwards they asked whether any more would go off. We signaled 'No,' and they immediately continued their work. Twice during that day they brought us food.

On the morning of the 21st, the commander commanded some of us by signs to bring the goods in our tent to him in order to have them sealed, which we did. Immediately, in our presence, they sealed our goods. While our men were sitting there, some thieves were brought in, who, during the salvage operation, had stolen some hides, iron and other things. The goods had been put on their backs and they were punished in our presence to show us that our goods were not to be plundered. They were beaten on the soles of their feet, with sticks about 1 meter long and as thick as the arm of an average boy. Some lost the toes off their feet. Each one received 30 or 40 strokes.

Around noon they signaled to us that we would be leaving. Those able to ride were given a horse and those who because of their injuries were unable to ride were carried in hammocks by order of the commander.

In the afternoon we set out with horsemen and soldiers as guards. We stayed overnight in the small town of *Taejong*. After having eaten something, all of us were brought to a warehouse where we were to sleep, but it looked more like a horsestable than an inn or dormitory. We had travelled about 4 mijl.[2]

On the 22nd, in the early morning, we continued on horseback. Our way passed by a small fortress, where we saw two war junks. There we had our morning meal. In the afternoon we arrived in the town of *Cheju*,[3] which is where the governor had his residence.[4] As soon as we arrived there, they assembled us on a field in front of the town hall. They gave each of us a cup of water in which rice had been boiled to drink[5] We thought this was going to be our last drink and that together we were going to die, so terrifying was the sight of guns and war material, as well as the display of all manner of dress. About 3000 armed men were standing there. We never had seen or heard of such behavior, either among the Chinese, or the Japanese.

Then, the book-keeper and the same three other persons who had been singled out before, were brought before the governor in the same way as we had earlier been brought before the commander. Thrown down, and lying there a moment, amidst shouting and pointing, we saw someone sitting like a king on a raised platform in front of the town hall. After we had been seated near him, he signalled to ask where we were from and where we wanted to go. We gestured and indicated as best we could the old answer: to Nagasaki in Japan. On which he nodded his head, showing that he must have understood something. Then the other men who could walk were brought over, four at a time, to His Excellency and interrogated. To each question, we answered with gestures as best we could, since we were unable to understand them or they us. Then the governor had all of us brought to a house which had been the residence of the uncle of the King until he died. He had been exiled to the island for trying to usurp the throne and banish the King from his country.[6]

The house was watched by a strong guard all around. We received for an allowance 3/4 catty[7] of rice and the same quantity of wheat-meal a day, but very little else to go with this, and what there was we could not eat. Thus we had to take our meals with salt and some water.

The governor was a good and understanding man, as we later found out. About 70 years old, he was from the royal city and held in great esteem at court. He let us know that he would write to the King and that he had to wait for an answer indicating what to do with us. The answer from the King was not quick in coming, since the distance to the capital is about 12 to 13 mijl by sea and then more than 70 mijl overland. We asked the governor if we could sometimes receive some meat and other side dishes, as we could no longer keep going on rice and salt. Also we asked for permission to stretch our legs, and to wash ourselves and the few clothes we had. This was granted to us; daily six men in turn were allowed to go out. And he ordered that side dishes be provided.

He often invited us to ask this or that in our language and to write something. Thus, finally, in a broken way we began to speak some words to one another. Also, he sometimes organized feasts and other entertainment to dispel our sadness. Every day he encouranged us, telling us that we could be sent to Japan once the answer from the King arrived. He also ordered our sick to be given treatment. Thus we were taken care of by a heathen in a way that would put many a Christian to shame.

On 29 October in the afternoon the book-keeper, the chief navigation officer and the under-surgeon[8] were called to the governor. Arriving there they found a man with a long red beard. The governor asked what kind of man he was, on which they answered, a Dutchman like us. Then the governor started laughing and signalled to say he was a Korean. After much talking and mutual gesturing, this man, who until then had been silent, asked us in a very broken way in our language what kind of people we were and where we were from. We answered him: "Dutchmen from Amsterdam." He then asked where we had come from and where we had been heading. We answered, from Taiwan, intending to go to Japan, but the Almighty had prevented this; we explained that we had been in a storm that lasted five days and fetched us up on the island, and that we were now praying for a merciful deliverance and help.

Our men asked him his name, what country he was from, and how he had arrived there. He answered: "My name is Jan Janse Weltevree, from De Rijp. In 1626 I left the fatherland on the ship *Hollandia* and in 1627 I was on the ship *Ouwerkerck* on the way to Japan. Contrary winds blew us near the coast of Korea and, since we needed drinking water, we went ashore with a boat. Three of us were captured by the inhabitants. The other men escaped with the boat and returned to our ship."[9] During the Manchu invasion, about 17 or 18 years before, his two companions had been killed. They were Dirck Gijsbertsz from De Rijp and Jan Pieterse Verbaest from Amsterdam. They had arrived in the Indies together with Weltevree.

Asked where he lived, what he did for a living, and why he had come to the island, he answered that he was living in the royal city (*Seoul*), that he received from the King a decent support of board and clothes, that he had been sent here to see what kind of people we were and how we had arrived here. He also told us that several times he had petitioned the King and the officials to be sent to Japan, but the King had always refused, answering: "If you were a bird, you could freely fly there. We do not send strangers away from our country. We will take care of you, giving you board and clothing, and thus you will have to finish your life in this country." He offered us much consolation and told us that if we should meet the King, we should not expect anything different. Thus the joy of meeting an interpreter nearly turned into sadness. It was surprising that this man, about 57 or 58 years old, had almost forgotten his mother tongue. At first, as was said, we could hardly understand him, but within a month of mixing with us he learned it again.

All of what we mentioned above and what happened to our ship and its people was carefully written down and read to us, translated by Jan Janszen, in order to be sent to the court on the first good wind.

The governor daily rallied our spirits, saying that an answer would not take long in coming and hoping that good tidings would come, so that we might be sent to Japan. We had to take comfort in this. He showed us nothing but friendship during this time. He allowed the oft-mentioned Weltevree, with one of his officers or upper "*benjoesen*"[10], to visit us daily in order to keep him informed about how we were doing.

At the beginning of December a new governor arrived; the three year term of his predecessor had expired. We were highly distressed and afraid that with the new lord would come new laws, which in fact occured. Before his departure the former governor ordered a long padded coat to be made for each one of us as well as a pair of long leather stockings and a pair of shoes with which to keep off the cold, for it had become colder and we possessed few clothes. He also handed us back our salvaged books.[11] He gave us a large jar of oil to be used during the wintertime. At his farewell dinner he feasted us well. Through the aforementioned Weltevree, he told us that he was very sad that he had not been able to send us to Japan, or take us with him to the continent, but that we ought not be sad about his departure. Once at the court, he would use every means and and make it his task to secure our liberation, or to get us off the island as soon as possible and bring us to the court. For all the courtesies he had shown us, we thanked His Excellency sincerely.

Once the new governor had taken up his office, he immediately took away all our side dishes; thus most of our meals were rice and salt, with only water to drink. We complained about this to the former governor, who because of contrary winds was still on the island. He answered that as his term had expired he could do nothing, but he wrote to the governor about it. Thus during the presence of the former governor, the new governor provided us now and then most soberly with side dishes to avoid further complaints.

1654

In early January the old governor left and our situation greatly worsened. Instead of rice we received barley and instead of wheat, barley meal, without any side dishes. Thus we had to sell our barley in order to get some side dishes. We had to be content with 3/4 catty of barley meal a day. But our outings of six men a day continued. Being miserable, we looked for any means to escape. With the coming of spring and the rainy season, the answer from the King was slow in coming, and we were very much afraid of being exiled on the island and having to finish our lives in imprisonment.

We were considering whether we might not escape in one of the sea-ready vessels that could be seen at night by the quay. An opportunity came at the end of April. Six of us, among whom were the chief navigation officer and three others (who years later did make it to Nagasaki), planned an escape. One of the group, climbing over a wall on his way to the vessel we had selected to see if the ebb tide had stopped, was forced to return because barking dogs made the guards ever more watchful. Our attempt came to nothing.

In the beginning of May our navigation officer with five men (among whom were the three mentioned),[12] going out in their turn, found near a small village just outside the city a vessel that had not been stripped of its seagoing equipment. There was no one around. Immediately, they sent one man home to get some plaited straw, made for such an occasion, and two small loaves of bread for each of them. Once again together, each one drank water, and without taking anything else, entered the vessel and pulled it over a sandbar towards the sea. Some onlookers from the village stood there very astonished, not knowing what was going on. Finally one villager entered a house and grabbed a musket, with which he ran into the water after those who were in the vessel. By this time, however, they had reached the open sea, except for one man who had not managed to reach the boat in time, being the one who had loosened the hawsers securing the vessel. He chose to return to shore. Those in the boat hoisted the sail, but since they were not familiar with the fittings, the mast fell overboard taking the sail with it. Exerting great effort, they were able to get the mast up again, securing it with the plaiting, and once again hoisted the sail. Then the wooden spur of the mast broke off. The mast and the sail fell overboard a second time. Unable to get it upright again, they floated back towards the coast. Those on land, observing this, immediately set out in another vessel to pursue them. When their pursuers drew alongside their vessel, our men jumped in this second boat and, although the pursuers had a gun, commenced throwing them overboard intending to continue in that vessel, but it was nearly full of water and unfit. And so they all returned to the shore, whence they were brought before the governor.

Each man was bound tightly to a heavy plank, one hand imprisoned by a clamp nailed to the plank[13], and a chain put around his neck. Thus fettered, they were thrown prostrate before the governor. The others were called from their house of captivity and brought before the governor as well, where they saw their mates lying in such misery.

The governor inquired whether they had acted with or without the knowledge of the others. They answered it had happened without their knowledge (in order to avoid further difficulties and to spare them from receiving the same punishment). Then the governor inquired what they had intended to do, to which they answered that they wanted to go to Japan. Then he asked if with such a small vessel, without water and so little bread, such was possible. To which they answered it would be better to die once and for all. Then they were released from their chains and each one received 25 strokes on the bare buttocks with paddles as wide as a hand and as thick as a finger, rounded on both sides and about a fathom long. After this, they had to keep to their beds for about a month. Our outings were forbidden, and we were all strictly guarded day and night.

This island, which they call *Cheju* and we call Quelpaert, lies, as aforementioned, on a latitude of 33 degrees 32 minutes and is about 12 to 13 mijl distant from the south corner of the mainland of Korea. On the inner side, or north coast, is a bay which their ships can enter and depart from, travelling to and from the mainland. For anyone who does not know the coast, the approach is very dangerous because of the invisible reefs which make many ships, should they miss the bay because of bad weather, turn to Japan, as there is no other place on the island to cast anchor, or to stay safely. All around the island there are many visible and invisible cliffs and reefs. It is densely populated and produces much food. There is an abundance of horses and cows, which provide large yearly revenues for the King. The inhabitants are common people and very poor, held in low esteem by people from the mainland[14]. There is one high mountain covered with trees (*Hallasan*), and other mountains that are mostly bare but with many valleys where rice is cultivated.

At the end of May the long expected news from the King arrived. To our sadness we had to go to the court, but to our joy we would be liberated from this oppressive prison. Six or seven days later, we were put aboard four separate junks where we each had our legs and one arm locked in a wooden block, as the authorities were concerned about us taking one or the other junk. We might have done so if we had been free and loose during this voyage, since most of the soldiers who escorted us were seasick. After having sat like that for two days, the junks unable to set sail because of contrary winds, we were freed and sent back to our prison-house. Four or five days later the wind was blowing well, and in the early morning we returned to our junks and were locked up and guarded as before. The anchor was weighed and when the sails were set, we left. In the evening we approached the mainland, where we laid at anchor. In the morning we were freed from our junks and we went ashore, well guarded by soldiers.

The next day we received horses and rode to a town called *Haenam*. Since each junk had arrived at a different place, we were not reunited, all thirty-six of us, until that evening.

The next day after having something to eat, we mounted our horses again and towards evening we arrived in a town called *Yŏngam*. That night Paulus Janse Cool, a gunner from Purmerend, died. Since we had lost our ship he had never been in good health. By order of the town commandant he was buried in our presence. From the graveside we left again on horseback and in the evening we arrived in a town called *Naju*.

The next morning we left again, and that night we spent in a town called *Changsŏng*. We left in the morning and that day passed a very high mountain on which a mountain fortress called *Ipamsansŏng* was situated.[15] We spent that night in *Chŏngŭp*. We left in the morning and the same day we arrived in the town of *T'aein*.

The next morning we were mounted on horseback again. At noon we arrived in a small town called *Kŭmku*. After having our noon meal there, we left again and towards evening we arrived in a big town called *Chŏnju*, where formerly the King used to hold his court. Now the governor of *Chŏlla* province lives there. Throughout the country, this city is famous as a commercial center. One cannot reach it by water; it is an inland city.

The next morning we left *Chŏnju* and in the evening arrived in a town called *Yosan*, which was the last town we stopped at in *Chŏlla* province.

The next morning we left again on horseback and in the evening we arrived in a small town called *Unjin* in the province of *Ch'ungch'ondo*.

The following day we left for a town called *Yŏnsan*. Having spent the night there, the next morning we were again on horseback and arrived in the evening in a town called *Kongju*, where the governor of that province resides.

The next day we crossed a big river and arrived in the province of *Kyŏnggido*, in which the royal city is situated.

After another few days of travel, spending the nights in several towns
and villages, we finally crossed a big river (*Han Gang*), about as large
as the River Maas at Dordrecht. We took a boat across the river and,
after riding about 1/2 mijl, we arrived at a very large walled city, called
Seoul, which is the residence of the King. (In all, we had travelled about
70 to 75 mijl, mostly northbound, with some inclination to the west).[16]

Having arrived in the city, we were kept all together in one house for
about two or three days. Then we were separated into groups of two,
three or four men and sent to the homes of Chinese who had fled their
own country. As soon as we were thus settled, we were brought before
the King (*Hyojong*), who questioned us about everything, thanks to the
help of the aforementioned Jan Janse Weltevree. Having answered him
the best we could, we explained to His Majesty that because of a storm
we had lost our ship, arrived in a strange country, been deprived of our
parents, wives, children, friends and fiancees, and we requested that the
King show us mercy and send us to Japan, to find our countrymen and
return to our fatherland. He answered us, through Weltevree, that it was
not his way to send strangers away from his land, and that we would
have to live there to the end of our days but that he would take care of
our support. Then he made us dance in the manner of our country, sing
and exhibit to him all kinds of things we had learned. Having treated us
well in his way, he presented each of us with two pieces of linen cloth to
clothe ourselves for the first time in the way of this country. Then we
were brought back to the houses where we slept.

The next day we were all called to present ourselves to the general
who told us, through the interpretation of the often mentioned Weltevree, that the King had made us his bodyguards. Every month we
would receive about 70 catties of rice. He gave each of us a round
wooden plaque on which our names (according to their writing), ages,
what kind of people we were [Hollanders], and the capacity in which we
were serving the King, were all cut out in characters and on which the
seal of the King and that of the general were burned.[17] Each of us
received a musket, powder and lead, and were ordered to demonstrate
our loyalty by appearing and bowing low before the general at every
new moon and every full moon. It is like that among them, the lesser

paid royal servants have to do this before their superiors, as do the members of the crown council before the King.

For six months every year the general and all those in royal service are in attendance at court and accompany the King. The men are drilled for three months in the spring and for three months in the autumn. Every month three trips are made, with exercises in shooting as in other arts of war. Finally, war exercises are held, as if all the weight of the world was resting on their shoulders. A Chinese guard (there are many Chinese serving as guards) and the often mentioned Weltevree were put in command of us to teach us everything in their (Korean) way and to supervise us. They gave each of us two small pieces of hemp cloth which we were to use to provide for our needs and to pay for the making of our clothes.

Daily we were bid to come to the homes of important people, since they as well as their wives and children were curious to see us. The common people of the island (*Cheju*) had spread rumours that we were more like monsters than people. They said that in order to drink something we had to place our noses behind our ears, and that since our hair was blond we looked more like underwater creatures than humans, and so on. The thing that highly astonished many upper class people and made them consider us better looking than the people of their own nation, was the fairness of our skin, which they like very much. All in all, in the beginning we hardly could use the narrow streets near where we lived, and even in our homes the crowds would not give us even a little rest. Finally, the general forbade us to visit anyone who had not received permission from him. Sometimes even slaves, without their masters knowing about it, would take us out of our homes and make fools of us.

In August the Manchu envoy arrived to collect his usual tribute.[18] The King sent us to a large fortress to stay there for as long as the Manchu envoy was in town.[19] This fortress is about 6 to 7 mijl away from the city, on a very high mountain, about 2 mijl along a steep, climbing road. It is a strong fortress in which the King takes refuge in time of war. The most important monks of the country reside there. There is always enough food for three years. Several thousand men can stay up there. The fortress is called *Namhansansŏng.*[20] We stayed there until 2 or 3 September, when the Manchu envoy had departed.

At the end of November it was freezing cold. The river about one mijl outside the city was frozen so hard that 200 to 300 fully loaded horses in a row could cross it. Early in December, the general, seeing that we were suffering from the cold and from poverty, informed the King about us. He ordered that some of the hides from our ship, wrecked on the shore on the island (*Cheju*), should be given to us. These hides had been dried and transported here by ship, though most were rotten and eaten by mites. (Hides were considered deteriorating goods by the United East India Company.) We were ordered to sell these hides and use the proceeds to provide ourselves with as much protection as possible against the cold. Instead, we agreed among ourselves to buy several small houses, each of which two or three persons could share. We wanted to get away from our landlords who harassed us daily to fetch wood. The misery of going back and forth more than 3 mijl across the mountains in a bitter cold we were quite unaccustomed to was hard for us to bear. We realized that except from God, there was no other solution to be hoped for, and we preferred suffering some cold to constantly being harrassed by these heathens (the Chinese landlords). We put together some 3 or 4 taels[21] of silver from each person, and we bought the small houses for 8 or 9 taels each (28 to 30 florins). The remaining money was used to buy some clothes and thus we spent the winter together.

1655

In March, as already mentioned, the Manchu envoy returned. We were ordered not to leave our homes. The day the Manchu envoy departed, our chief navigation officer, Hendrick Janse, from Amsterdam and a gunner, Hendrick Janse Bos, from Haarlem pretended they were in need of firewood and went to the woods, hiding near the road along which the Manchu envoy had to pass. The moment he passed by, accompanied by some hundreds of horsemen and soldiers, our men broke through the ranks and grabbed the horse of the highest dignitary by the head. Having thrown off their Korean clothes, they stood before the Manchu envoy dressed as Dutchmen (which clothes they were wearing underneath their Korean clothes), immediately creating such a commotion that there was a great stir.

The Manchu envoy asked what kind of people they were, but they could not understand one another. He ordered our navigation officer to come with him to the place where he was going to spend the night.[22] He asked those who accompanied him if there was no interpreter who could understand the navigation officer. The often mentioned Weltevree was ordered by the King to come immediately.

We too were taken from our neighbourhood and brought to the court of the King. Having been brought before the state councillors, we were asked if we knew about this, to which we answered that it had happened without our knowledge. Notwithstanding, they ordered us to be punished with 50 strokes on the buttocks, since we had not warned them that our two companions had gone out. The King was constantly informed about everything, and he did not consent to the beatings, saying we had come to his country because of a storm and not to rob or steal. He ordered us to be sent home and to stay there until further notice.

After the navigation officer[23] and Weltevree had arrived at the place the Manchu was at and the officer had been interviewed about everything, the matter was settled by the King and the councillors. The Manchu envoy was to be bribed for an amount of money in order not to mention the matter to the great Khan. They were afraid that the guns as well as the goods they had salvaged (from *Cheju*) would be demanded as tribute. Our two companions, our chief navigator and the gunner, were sent back to the city and were immediately put in jail, where they died after some time. We never heard for certain whether they had died a natural death or were beheaded, since we were never allowed to visit them; this was forbidden.[24]

In June the Manchu envoy was expected again. We were all called to appear before the general, where Weltevree informed us in the name of the King that another ship had been reported wrecked on Quelpaert Island, and that Weltevree, given his age, was unable to go there. Thus, three of our men who spoke Korean the best had to go down to ask what kind of ship this was. Two or three days later an assistant, a gunner and a sailor went down, accompanied by a Korean sergeant.[25]

In August, we were informed that the two prisoners had died and that the Manchu envoy was arriving again. We were well guarded in our houses and under threat of corporal punishment. We were forbidden to go out before the Manchu had been gone two or three days. Just before the arrival of the Manchu envoy we received a letter, handed over to us, from our three companions. They informed us that they were in a fortress in the extreme southern corner of the country, that they were under strict guard, and that they had been sent there in case the Manchu Khan had discovered our presence and claimed us. In that case the governor would have written that they had gone to the island and en route had been shipwrecked, thus hiding their presence and keeping them in the country.[26]

Towards the end of the year, the Manchu envoy came again, across the ice, to collect his tribute. As before, the King ordered us to be well guarded.

1656

Since the Manchu had been back twice without mentioning us, in the beginning of the year some members of the state council and other prominent people, who were fed up with our presence, urged the King to do away with us. For three days the authorities discussed this. The King, the brother of the King, a general and some other important people who sympathized with us were very much against this. The general proposed it would be better, instead of killing us, to let each one of us fight with equal arms against two Koreans, letting the fight last until we all were dead, by which the King would not be known among his people to have strangers publicly killed. All this was secretly told us by friendly people. During these discussions we were ordered not to leave our houses. Not knowing what was threatening us, we talked about this with Weltevree, who simply answered: "If you people live three more days, you'll live longer." The brother of the King presided over these meetings, and on his way to and on his way back he had to pass through our neighbourhood. When we saw him, we fell down in front of him, highly complaining to him. He told the King about it. In this way, thanks to the King and his brother, against the agitation of many, our lives were saved.

Because of the urging of those who were not in favour of us, claiming that we would approach the Manchu envoy again, which would of course create difficulties, the King decided to exile us to *Chŏlla* province, to our joy, for we were saved. The King would give us 50 catties of rice per month from his own income.

In early March we left the royal city on horseback. We were seen off by the oft-mentioned Weltevree and other acquaintances, who accompanied us as far as the river, about one mijl outside the city. When we were embarked on the scow, Weltevree returned to the city. This was the last time we ever saw him or heard reliable news of him.

We travelled down the same road we had taken on our inward journey, passing through the same towns. From place to place food and horses were provided at government expense, as had been the case on our inward journey. Finally we arrived in the town of *Yŏngam*, where we spent the night.

In the morning we departed and in the afternoon arrived in a large town with a fortress, called *Taechang* (big granary), or *Cholla Pyŏngyŏng* (Cholla garrison), where the *pyŏngsa*, the commander of the provincial military, who is first in authority after the governor, has his residence. We were handed over by the sergeant, together with the letters from the King to the commandant. The sergeant was immediately ordered to fetch our three companions, who last year had been sent away from the royal city and to bring them here. They were in a fortress where the vice-admiral resides, about 12 mijl away.[27] We were immediately given a local house, where we could live together. Three days later, our three companions joined us and we were 33 men altogether.

In April we received some hides, which had remained so long on the island (*Cheju*), that they were not valuable enough to be transported to the royal city. Since we were here not more than about 18 mijl from the island, close to the seacoast, they could easily be brought here. With these hides we could obtain ourselves some clothes and get some necessities for our new lodging. The commandant ordered us to clean the square, or market place, in front of the town hall twice a month, pulling out the grass and keeping it neat.

1657

In the beginning of the year the commandant, because of some mistakes committed in his service to the country, was called away by order of the King. He was in great peril of his life. He was much loved by the ordinary people. Because of high-level intervention and his high birth, the King pardoned him and promoted him to a more important post. For us, as well as for the inhabitants, he had been a very good man.

In February we got a new commandant. He was not like his predecessor. He very often made us work. The former one had provided us with wood for burning, but the new one took this privilege away and we had to cut our own. In order to get it, we had to go as far as 3 mijl over the mountains. This was very irksome. But in September we were freed from him. He died of a heart attack, which made us and his own people rejoice very much because he had been a harsh ruler.

In November the court sent us a new commandant who did not care about us at all. When we mentioned to him our need of clothes and the like he answered that the King had given no order except to provide us with our portion of rice. Other necessities we would have to get for ourselves. Since our clothes were worn from the continual gathering of wood and the cold winter was at hand, realising that these people were very curious and very eager to hear something exotic and that over there begging is no shame, our distress forced us to beg. We accepted and put up with that profession. With that and with our remaining rations and other necessities, we could provide for ourselves against the cold. Since, in order to get a handful of salt which we ate with our rice, we often had

to walk more than half a mijl, we presented a request to the commandant. We asked his permission to leave for 3 or 4 days in turn. Because
of gathering wood and selling it to the people, our clothes were worn
out, having been used so long, and because we were mostly eating no
more than rice and salt and a drink of water, we were very miserable and
everything was a heavy burden to us, we wanted to try our luck with the
farmers and with the monks in the monasteries (of which there are many
over there), in order to live through the winter. He agreed, and by these
means we obtained some clothes and we could pass the winter.

1658

In the beginning of the year the commandant was called away and a
new one was appointed in his place. The new one wanted to prevent our
going out and proposed to give us instead three pieces of linen every
year, for which we would have to work every day. But we would have
needed more for our clothes, besides our need for side dishes, wood and
other needs. Moreover, that was a bad year for cereals and everything
was costly, so we declined this politely, requesting that he would give us
15 or 20 days leave in turns. To this he consented. Moreover, since
typhoid fever had broken out among us, of which they have a great dis-
like, he ordered that those who remained should take care of the sick
while those going out should avoid going in or near the royal city
(*Seoul*) or the Japanese settlement.[28] We also had to take care of pulling
out the grass and sometimes some odd jobs.

1659

In April, the King[29] died and with the consent of the Manchus his son
became King in his place. We continued and managed as we used to do.
We found our best chances with the monks, since they are very generous
and they liked us very much, especially when we would tell about the
manners of our country and about other nations. They are very eager to
hear about life in other countries. If it had been up to them, they would
have listened to us whole nights long.

1660

In the beginning of the first year (of the new King), we were freed of our commandant and immediately a new one took his place. The new one was very sympathetic to us. He often said that if he had his way, or if it were in his power, he would have us sent back to our country, to our parents and relatives. He gave us our freedom and the burden put on us by his two predecessors was lifted.

This year the harvest of grains and other crops was very bad.

1661

Since it did not rain, the harvest of grains and other crops was very bad.

1662

This year, until the new plants came out, was even worse. Thousands of people died of hunger. It was difficult to make use of the roads, as there were many highwaymen. By order of the King, strong guards were stationed on all roads to protect travellers as well as to bury the dead who, because of the famine, were dying along the highways, and at the same time to prevent murder and robbery as this was practised daily. Several towns and villages were plundered. Royal warehouses[30] were broken open and the grain looted, without catching the criminals, as it was mostly done by the slaves of important people. In order to keep alive, ordinary people and the poor mostly ate acorns, the inner bark of pine trees and wild vegetables.

*   *   *

Now we will tell a bit about the whereabouts of the country and the manner of its people. (See *A Description of the Kingdom of Korea* below)

*   *   *

1663

The hard times had lasted now more than three years. Many people had died. Ordinary men had no income, as we mentioned before. However one town might have somewhat more crops than another, especially those situated in the lowlands, or near rivers and marshlands; there one always could produce some rice. Without that, the whole country would almost have died out. In the beginning of this year our commandant, who no longer could provide our portions of rice, wrote about this to the governor. Without the knowledge of the King, who provided our rations out of the royal revenues, he could not transfer us to another place.

At the end of February the commandant received an order to split us up among three different towns: twelve men to *Yŏsu*[31], five men to *Sunch'ŏn*[32] and five men to *Namwon*.[33] We were twenty two men in all.[34] We were highly distressed about this separation. Here we had been rather well settled, according to the fashion of the country, with houses, furniture and small gardens. All this had been obtained with great pain and now we would have to leave it all. It would not be easy to be as comfortable again, arriving in a new town, given the hard times. But this sadness changed into great joy for those who were saved (that is, those who escaped to Japan).

In early March, after taking leave of the commandant and thanking His Excellency for the good treatment and friendship we had received from him, each one left for his town. The commandant provided horses for the transport of the sick and for our few belongings. Those in good health had to walk. The ones for *Sunch'ŏn* and *Yŏsu* took the same road. The first evening we arrived in a town where we spent the night, the second night in another town, and the fourth day we arrived in *Sunch'ŏn* which we left the next day, leaving behind the five men who were appointed to stay there. We stayed overnight in a state warehouse. At sunrise we left and around 9 o'clock we arrived in *Yŏsu*. The servant of the governor who accompanied us brought us to the commandant, or admiral of the province of *Chŏlla,* who resides there. He immediately provided us with a house with some furniture and gave us the same ration as we used to receive. He seemed a good and gentle person, but two days after our arrival he left.

Three days after his departure a new commandant arrived to take his place, which turned out to be an ordeal for us. Every day we had to stand ready, in the summer in the hot sun, in the winter in the rain, hail and snow, from early morning till evening. When the weather was fine we did nothing but pick up arrows, because servants and subordinates did nothing but daily exercise in shooting with bow and arrow in order to be the best archer.[35] And he charged us with more work, pestering Christian men, for which the Almighty made him pay, as we will tell later on. We plodded on together, with great sadness. The winter now being at hand, we had no extra clothes because of the bad years. Our companions in the two other towns had, because of the good crops there, the possibility of clothing themselves a little better than we could. This we presented to the commandant, asking if for three days, half of our men could take care of our duties, while the others went around to find provisions and thus continue in turns, thinking that this would do. It turned out quite well. The important people pitied us very much, resulting in the circumstance that they often closed their eyes to the terms, and so we could be away 15 to 30 days. What we could collect was shared equally among us. We continued to do this until the departure of the commandant.

1664

In the beginning of this year the term of our commandant expired. The King appointed him to the post of general, second in command in the province. Thus we got a new commandant, who immediately freed us of all burdens and ordered that we should not do more than our people in the other towns; that is to say, twice a month we had to muster, and we had to take care of our house in turns. On leaving we had to ask permission and let the secretary know, if need be, where we could be found.

We gave thanks to the good God for having been delivered of such a cruel man and having received in his place such a good man. The new man did but good to us. He showed us great friendship. He often sent for us, giving us food and drink, always pitying us. Often he asked us, why, living at the seaside, did we not try to go to Japan? On which we always answered that the King would not permit us, that we did not know the way and also that we did not have a boat to run away with. To which he replied, as if there were not enough vessels at the seashore. To which we replied that they did not belong to us. And if we failed, the King would punish us, not only for escaping, but also for taking someone else's boat. We said this in order not to arouse suspicion. Whenever we said so, His Excellency laughed very much. Now, seeing some chance, we did all we could to obtain a vessel, but we never were able to buy one, since the purchase always fell through because of some jealous people.[36]

The late commandant, after having been for about six months in his new post, had been summoned by order of the King to the court, because of his severe government. Making no exception for nobles or commoners, for any small affair he had let them be beaten unto death. Because of this, at the court he was beaten 90 strokes on the shins and then banished for life.

At the end of the year we saw first one star with a tail and then two stars with a tail: the first one in the South East, which one could see during about two months, the other one in the South West, with their tails pointing at one another.[37] This caused such a commotion at the court, that the King ordered all seaports and warjunks to be prepared, as well as food and ammunition to be provided to all the fortifications. Horsemen and soldiers had to exercise daily, thinking about nothing else than that something was about to happen. In the evening it was forbidden to light any light, inside the homes as well as outside along the seacoast. Ordinary people spent almost everything they had, keeping just enough to live until the next rice harvest. Moreover, since similar signs in the sky had occurred when the Manchus occupied the country,[38] as well as when the Japanese began the war with Korea, people were still afraid. Continually, important people and common people asked us what people in our country said if such a sign was seen, to which we answered that with us such was assumed to be a sign of punishment from heaven and in general foreboding war, hard times and malignant diseases, with which they agreed.[39]

1665

This year we plodded on. We did our best to obtain a boat, but we were always thwarted. We had a small boat though, with which we could get some food for side dishes and go around the islands in order to look out for the possibility that the Almighty at some time still might accord us deliverance.

Our comrades in the two other towns had, with the coming and going of their commandants, some easy times and some hard times, because their commandants were like ours, some good and some angry. But we all had to put up with this, realising that we were poor prisoners in a heathen country, thanking God that they kept us alive and that they gave us enough so that we would not die of hunger.

1666

In the beginning of this year we lost our good friend again, since his term had expired and the King bestowed a higher post on him. During these two years he had shown us much friendship. He also was much beloved by townsmen and farmers because of his goodness, and the King and the important people esteemed his good government and the knowledge he had. The houses in the town as well as in the countryside had been much improved by him, as well as the seafront and the war junks, during the time he had spent here. All this was highly appreciated at the court; the King endowed him with a good office.[40]

As the sea coast should not be without a commander, and the former one could not leave before the arrival of the new one, the new commandant arrived three days later. According to the indications of the fortune-tellers it was a favourable day to start his term of office in town. The new commandant wanted to teach us a lesson, as the previously mentioned exiled commandant had taught us. But his reign did not last long. He wanted us to pound rice every day, to which we answered that this and similar activities had not been imposed on us by the last commandant. Our portion being scarcely sufficient, we had enough to do to beg in order to get clothes and other necessities, and the King had not sent us

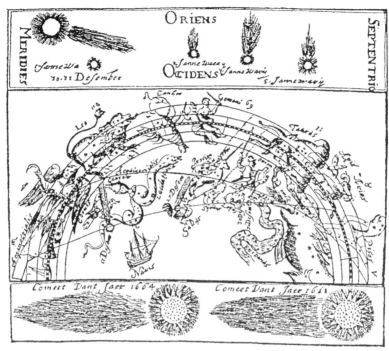

The comet at the end of the year 1664, compared with the one in 1618.
Hollandse Mercurius XV, April 1665

The comet observed
over Amsterdam 1664.
Hollands Mercurius XV

here to work. If we had to work for it, we would rather not receive our portion; then we would be free to see how we could get our own food and clothing, or to go to Japan, or to our country. We used other similar arguments as well, but he did not answer us. He ordered us to leave, saying that he was busy putting his affairs in order, by which we had to abide.

But quickly things turned out differently. Soon afterwards there was going to be a naval exercise and drill. Through the negligence of the constable, a box of gunpowder,[41] which is always kept before the mast, caught fire, blowing off the front of a junk and killing five men. The commandant meant to conceal this accident from the governor, but it turned out differently. The King has his spies all through the country. They are always around and they informed the governor of the province, who wrote directly to the court. By order of the King, the commandant was recalled. He was punished by 90 strokes on the shins and was banished for life, most of all because he had tried to suppress the facts and had dealt with the accident himself without informing his superiors.

Another commandant arrived in July. Like his predecessor he wanted to put us under a heavy workload. He wanted each of us to make 100 fathoms of straw rope every day. We told him that this was impossible for us and, as we had his predecessor, we told him our proposals. But he threatened to put us to another kind of work if we could not do that work. If his predecessor had not become powerless he too would have made us work. We realised that slavery was awaiting us if he managed to put us to doing this work and his successors would certainly continue likewise since, once a practice has been introduced by a commandant, it is not easily abolished, as we knew all too well from the town of *Pyŏngyŏng*, the labour and the pulling out of the grass; and we would have continued attending and picking up arrows, if we had not had such an exceptional commandant during whose time we had done our best to accumulate enough to be able to pay twice or threefold for a boat, as normally it would not be easy for us to get one.

Thus we looked for any means in the world to obtain a boat. We would rather try our chance once than constantly live in sorrow, sadness and in slavery in this heathen nation, brought on us every day by a crowd of spiteful people.

We finally agreed to ask our neighbour, a Korean and a good friend, who daily came to our house and often shared food and drinks with us. We decided to gull him and make him buy a boat under the pretext of gathering cotton wool on the islands, promising him more benefits once we returned from begging cotton wool. We did this to encourage him to buy a ship; we would reward him even better. He immediately made his inquiries and bought a vessel from a fisherman. We paid him the amount and he handed us the boat. The seller, upon hearing that the boat was for us, stopped the sale, since it was done by someone else and he said we would escape with his boat for which he would be killed, which certainly would be true. But we satisfied him by paying twice the value. He, thinking more about the money than about the trouble awaiting him, and we, seeing the chance we had, came to an agreement.

Immediately we provided the boat with a sail, anchor and ropes, oars and everything else needed in order to get away during the first quarter of the new moon. When the season is turning,[42] this is the best moment. We prayed that the Almighty would be our Guide.

Two of our mates, the under-surgeon Mattheus Eibocken and Cornelis Dirckse, who by chance were visiting us from *Sunch'ŏn*, as we used to visit one another, to whom we disclosed our plans, immediately agreed to join us. One of us, Jan Pieterse, living in *Sunch'ŏn*, being an experienced navigator, was sent for in order to warn him that all was finished and ready. When our messenger arrived in *Sunch'ŏn*, Pieterse turned out to be visiting our people in the town of *Namwon*, about 15 mijl away. Immediately he went up there to get him. Four days later he returned with Jan Pieterse. During that time he had covered about 50 mijl.[43]

Then together we deliberated thoroughly and on 4 September we had everything ready, including wood for burning. We were to leave with the setting of the moon, lifting anchor before the ebbtide came in, and continuing in the name of God, since there was already some murmuring among our neighbours.

In order to rouse less suspicion among the neighbours, we spent the night together cheerfully, meanwhile the rice, water and cooking pans and what more was needed during the voyage were brought to the boat by climbing over the town wall. When the moon went down we went over the wall into our boat with which we went to an island, about a cannon shot away, to get some drinking water. After having provided ourselves with water, we had to pass right by the boats of the town and the war junks. Having passed these, we went downwind and the current helped us. Then we installed the sail and left the bay. Around daybreak we passed a vessel that hailed us, yet we did not answer, afraid it might have been a guard.

The next day, 5 September, at sunrise the wind fell still. We lowered our sail and started rowing, afraid they might pursue us and that the sail would betray us. Towards noon the weather cooled off a bit from the West. We set our sail again, keeping our course S.E. by guessing. Towards evening it became quite cool from the same direction. The last point of Korea was now behind us and we were no longer afraid of being caught.

September 6, in the morning we were close to one of the first Japanese islands. We kept the same wind and speed. In the evening we were close by the island of Firando (*Hirado*), as the Japanese later explained to us. Since none of us had ever been to Japan, the coast was unknown to us and the Koreans had not been able to instruct us correctly. They had told us that no islands should be at starboard in order to arrive in Nagasaki. So we turned around. At first the island looked very small. That night we remained on the west coast of the island.

September 7, it was getting cooler with variable winds and we sailed along the islands (we learned then that there were a number of islands next to one another). We tried to stay away from these. In the evening we sculled towards an island in order to anchor there overnight, since there was a lot of wind, but we saw so many torches on the small islands that we thought it better to remain under sail. With a cold wind behind us, we sailed the whole night through.

September 8, we found ourselves in the same place we had been in the evening. The sea current must have caused this. Again we took to the sea in order to get away from the islands. About two mijl out, a cold wind turned against us. We had more than enough to do with our small and simple boat to reach the coast and to look for a bay, since the wind was getting stronger and stronger. In the middle of the afternoon we arrived in a bay and cast our anchor. There we cooked some food and ate without knowing what islands these were. Sometimes people passed in their boats without paying any attention to us.

Towards evening the weather calmed down. A boat with six men in it, each with a dagger on both sides passed us close by sculling. They put one person on shore across the bay. When we saw this we immediately weighed the anchor, hoisted our sail, and tried sculling and sailing to get back into the sea, but we were followed and overtaken by that boat. If the wind had not been against us and if several other boats in the bay had not come to assist the first one, we would have been able to hold them off with sticks and bamboo poles we had made into pikes, but seeing that they looked like Japanese, according to what we had heard and that they were pointing towards the place they wanted us to go, we raised the small flag of the Prince (narrow stripes of orange/red, white and blue), which we had made in order to show it if we happened to land on a Japanese island.

We shouted: *"Hollando, Nangasaki!"* They signaled us to lower the sail and scull backwards, which we did immediately as if we were captured. They came on board and took the man who sat at the helm in their boat. Shortly afterwards they towed us in front of a village, where they used a large anchor and thick ropes to moor us well and with guarding barques they kept us. Another of our men joined the helmsman and both were brought ashore and interrogated. But they could not understand one another. Ashore there was a great stir. It seemed that there was not one man without one or two daggers at his side. We looked at one another with sadness in our eyes, thinking, "this is it." They pointed towards Nagasaki and meant to show that our ships and our people were there. This consoled us somewhat, but we were not without suspicion that we were trapped and could not escape and they just wanted to satisfy us.

In the night, a large barque rowed into the bay and we were brought

on board where we met the official who was third in authority in the
islands (we realized this once we were in Nagasaki). He said that he
knew us and that we were Dutchmen. He gestured and pointed that there
were five ships in Nagasaki; that he would bring us there in four or five
days; that we would be satisfied; that the islands were the *Goto* islands;
that the inhabitants were Japanese under the authority of the emperor.
They asked where we were from, to which we answered and gestured as
well as possible that we came from Korea, that 13 years ago our ship
had been lost on an island and that we now tried to go to Nagasaki to
join our people. Then our mood lightened a bit, but still it was mixed
with fear since the Koreans had told us that all strangers coming to the
Japanese islands were beaten to death. We had sailed about 40 mijl on
an unknown course with our simple, little and old vessel.

September 9, 10 and 11 we remained at anchor, being well guarded on
our boat as well as on land. They provided us with food, water, wood
and other things needed. Since it was raining steadily they covered our
boat with small straw mats in order to keep us dry.

September 12, they provided us with everything needed for the voyage to Nagasaki. In the afternoon we weighed anchor and towards
evening we stopped at the other side of the island in front of a village,
where we spent the night.

September 13, at sunrise the official got in his barque, carrying some
letters and goods destined for the imperial court. We weighed our
anchors, being in convoy with two big boats and two small ones. Our
two mates who had been brought on land were on one of the large boats.
They joined us only in Nagasaki.

Towards evening we were in front of the bay and around midnight we
laid at anchor on the Roads of Nagasaki. There we saw the five ships as
we had been told before. The inhabitants and the authorities from *Goto*
had done us only good, without demanding anything in return from us.
We presented them with some rice, since we had nothing else to offer,
but they refused to accept this.

September 14, in the morning we were all brought ashore and wel-
comed by the Company's interpreter, who interrogated us about everything. Once everything was written down, it was handed to the governor.

Towards noon we were brought before the governor who asked us the following questions, which we answered as written. The governor praised us very much for having searched and found liberty across such a wide water with great danger, with such a small, old and simple boat. He ordered the interpreters to bring us to the island (*Deshima*), to the Opperhoofd. Arriving there, His Excellency Willem Volger, the Opperhoofd, Mr. Nicolaes de Roeij, second-in- command and the other wardens received us well and provided us once more with clothes in our fashion.

For all this in thankfulness may the Almighty grant happy blessings and lasting health. We could not thank the good Lord enough for having delivered us from imprisonment, with so much sadness and peril lasting 13 years and 28 days. Wishing that the eight companions who remained there likewise might be granted deliverance, may the Almighty grant his help.

*   *   *

October 1, Mr. Volger left the island and on October 23 he left with seven ships from the bay. We followed the ships with our eyes in sadness, since we had expected to be able to sail with His Excellency to Batavia. But the governor of Nagasaki kept us one more year.

October 25, the interpreter picked us up from the island and brought us to the governor, who asked each one of us personally the before mentioned questions. Then we were brought back to the island by the interpreters.

*   *   *

Questions asked by the governor of Nagasaki upon our first arrival and the answers which those of us, named below, gave in reply.

1. What kind of people were we and whence had we come?

    We were Dutchmen and came from Korea.

2. How had we come there and by what ship?

    On 16 August 1653 we had lost our ship the *Sperwer* because of a storm that lasted five days.

3. Where had we been shipwrecked and how many men and cannons had we?

    On the island we call Quelpaert and the Koreans call *Cheju*. We were 64 men and had 30 pieces.

4. How far is the island Quelpaert from the mainland and what is its situation?

    It lies about 10 to 12 mijl south of the mainland. It is densely populated and fertile, and about 15 mijl in circumference.

5. Where had we come from with our ship, and where had we stopped en route?

    We had left Batavia on 18 June for Taiwan with Mr. Caesar aboard who was to replace Mr. Verburgh as governor.

6. What was our cargo and where were we bound, and at that time who was the Opperhoofd here?

    We came from Taiwan, heading for Japan. We were laden with deer-skin, sugar, alum and other goods. At the time, Mr. Coijet was acting Opperhoofd.

7. What remained of the men, cargo and guns?

Twenty-eight men died. Goods and guns were lost. Afterwards some items of little importance were salvaged, but we did not know anything about the disposal of these items.

8. What did they do with us after the loss of the ship?

They put us in a prison house, they did but good to us and gave us food and drink.

9. Had we had any orders to capture Chinese or other junks, or to pillage the Chinese coast?

We had no other order than to proceed directly to Japan. Because of the storm we fell upon the coast of Korea.

10. Did we have on our ship any Christians, or any other nationality but Dutch?

None but employees of the Company.

11. How long had we remained on the island and where had we been taken from there?

After having been for about 10 months on the island we were summoned by the King to the court, which is in the city of *Seoul*.

12. How far is the city of *Seoul* from *Cheju* and how long were we on the way?

As already stated *Cheju* lies about 10 to 12 mijl from the mainland. We travelled then another 14 days on horseback. The total distance over water and land is about 90 mijl.

13. How long had we lived in the royal city and what had we done

there? What had the King given us for support?

We lived in their manner for three years and were employed as bodyguards for the general. We each received 70 catties of rice per month as a ration, along with some supplies of clothes.

14. For what cause had the King sent us away and to where?

Because our senior navigator and one other man had run off to the Manchu envoy in order to return to our nation by way of China, although with no success, the King banished us to the province of *Chŏlla.*

15. What happened to the men who had run to the Manchu envoy?

They were immediately jailed. We were not sure whether they were executed, or whether they died natural deaths. We never were able to learn with certainty.

16. Would not we know how large the land of Korea is?

According to our guess Korea is about 140 to 150 mijl long from South to North, and 70 to 80 mijl wide from East to West. It is divided into eight provinces and there are 360 towns, with many islands large and small.

17. Had we seen any Christians, or other foreign nationals there?

None but one Dutchman, Jan Janse, who heading from Taiwan with a ship in 1627, had been driven onto the coast by a storm, and who for lack of water went ashore with a boat, they were three men, there they were captured. His two companions had died in a battle when the Manchu invaded the country. There also were some Chinese who had fled there from their land on account of a war.

18. Was the said Jan Janse still alive and where did he live?

We do not know with certainty whether he is still alive, since we have not seen him in 10 years, since he lived at the court. It is said by some that he is still living and by others that he has died.

19. What about their weapons and military equipment?

Their arms are muskets, swords, bows and arrows. They also have few small spears.

20. Are there castles or fortresses in Korea?

The towns have light fortifications. There are some fortresses high up in the mountains to which they flee in time of war, these are always kept supplied with provisions for three years.

21. What kind of war junks do they have at sea?

Each town must maintain a war junk at sea. Each one is manned by two or three hundred men, both oarsmen as well as soldiers. These boats carry small guns.

22. Do they wage war, or must they offer tribute to any kings?

They wage no wars. The Manchu envoy comes two or three times a year to collect tribute. They also send tribute to Japan, though we do not know how much.

23. What kind of faith do they have and did they ever try to convert us?

As far as we could tell they have the same faith as the Chinese. Their custom is to draw no one to them, but to leave each person to his own opinion.

24. Are there many temples and statues? And how are they administered?

In the mountains are many temples and monasteries in which stand many statues. They are worshipped, as we think, in the Chinese manner.

25. Are there many monks, and how are they shaved and dressed?

There are monks in abundance, who must earn their livelihood by work and begging. They are dressed and shaved like the Japanese monks.

26. How are gentry and common people dressed?

Most are dressed in the Chinese manner. They wear hats of horse-hair, or cowhair, as well as those made of bamboo. They wear stockings and shoes.

27. Do they produce much rice and other cereals?

In the South rice and other grains grow in abundance in wet years, since their crops depend very much on rain. In dry years there are great famines. In the drought of 1660, 1661 and 1662, several thousands of people died. There is also a lot of cotton grown. But in the North they must make do with barley and millet, since no rice can grow there because of the cold.

28. Are there many horses and cows?

There are horses in abundance. Cows have been greatly diminished in the last two or three years by a contagious disease, which continues even now.

29. Do any foreign nations come to Korea for trade, or do the Koreans carry on any trade elsewhere?

Nobody carries on trade but this country (Japan), which has a lodge there. The Koreans carry on trade with the northern part of China and Peking.

30. Had we ever been in the Japanese trading post?

Such was expressly forbidden to us.

31. How do they trade among themselves?

    In the capital the upper classes do much business with silver. Common people and those in other towns trade with pieces of linen, according to its value and also with rice and other cereals.

32. What trade do they have with China?

    They carry there ginseng, silver and other goods, for which they obtain goods like those we bring to Japan, as well as silk.

33. Are there silver mines, or other mines?

    Several years ago they opened some silver mines, from which the King took one fourth. We have not heard of any other mines.

34. How do they find the ginseng root, what do they do with it, and where do they export it?

    Ginseng is found in the northern parts and is used by them as a medicine. Every year it is sent to the Manchus as tribute and merchants export it to China and Japan.

35. Had we ever heard whether China and Korea are linked overland?

    As we had been told, they are linked overland by a high mountain. In the winter it is dangerous to cross because of the cold and in the summer because of the wild beasts. Therefore people go mainly by sea, and in the winter over the ice which is more sure.

36. How are governors appointed in Korea?

    Every year all provincial governors are replaced and common magistrates every three years.

37. How long did we live together in *Chŏlla* province, and where did we get our food and clothes? How many of us had died there?

    We lived together for about seven years in the town of *Pyŏngyŏng*.

They gave us each month 50 catties of rice. We had to procure our clothes and food for side dishes from generous people. Eleven men died during that period.

38. Why had we been sent to other places, and what were the names of these places?

   During the years 1660, 1661 and 1662 no rain had come and one single town could not supply our ration. The King divided us in the last year to three different towns: 12 men to *Yŏsu,* 5 men to *Sunch'ŏn* and 5 men to *Namwon,* all towns in *Chŏlla.*

39. How big is the province of *Chŏlla* and where is it located?

   It is the southern province and has 52 towns. It is the most populous province of all and yields of food are excellent.

40. Had the King sent us away or had we run away?

   We knew quite well that the King would not send us away. Since we saw an opportunity for the eight of us to get away, we decided to do so, as we preferred to die once, than to live always in worry in that heathen land.

41. How many of us were still alive, and had we run away with or without the knowledge of the others?

   We were still 16 men alive. Among the 8 of us we had resolved this without talking about it beforehand with the others.

42. Why did we not tell them?

   Because we could not go all together, since every first and fifteenth of each month some of us had to appear before the magistrate of our city and we had permission to be away in turns.

43. How could these people get here as well?

   Only if the emperor [Shogun] would write to the King, then they might come here to us. The King would not dare to refuse such a request, since the emperor sends back his shipwrecked people every year.

44. Had we run away on other occasions, and why did we fail twice?

This was our third attempt. The first two times we had failed, first on Quelpaert island, since we did not understand the structure of their boats and the mast broke twice. The second attempt was in the royal city with the Manchu envoy, who was bribed by the King.

45. Had we never requested the King to send us away and why had he refused this?

Often we had asked the King and the state councillors, to which they always answered that they would not send foreigners out of the country, because they did not want their country to be known by other nations.

46. How did we get our boat?

We procured enough to put aside in order to buy the boat.

47. Had we had other boats besides this one?

This was our third one, but the others were too small to use for escaping to Japan.

48. From where had we run away and had we lived there?

From *Yŏsu* (*Chwasuyŏng*) where five of us were living and three from *Sunch'ŏn*.

49. How far is it from there and how long had we been underway?

Yŏsu according to our guess is about 50 mijl from *Nagasaki*. It took us three days to get to *Goto*. We stayed four days on *Goto* and it took us two days to get from *Goto* to here. Nine days altogether.

50. Why had we come to *Goto* and why had we tried to get away when the Japanese approached us?

    We were forced by a storm to shelter there. When the weather turned better we tried to continue our voyage to *Nagasaki*.

51. How had the people from *Goto* behaved themselves and how had they treated us? Had they claimed anything from us, or received anything?

    They took two of us ashore. They did us nothing but good, without claiming or receiving anything from us.

52. Had any of us ever been in Japan and how did we know the way?

    Nobody. Some Koreans who had been to *Nagasaki* had indicated the direction. And we still had the course as told to us by the navigation officer somewhat in our memory.

53. The men who were still in Korea — what were their names, their ages, in what capacities had they sailed, and where were they living now?

Johannis Lampen, assistant	age 36
Hendrick Cornelissen, 2nd boatswain	age 37
Jan Claeszen, cook	age 49

    Living in the town of Namwon.

Jacob Janse, quartermaster	age 47
Anthonij Uldircksen, gunner	age 32
Claes Arentszen, ship's boy	age 27

    Living in the town of Yŏsu.

Sander Boesquet, gunner	age 41
Jan Janse Spelt, junior boatswain	age 35

    (Living in the town of Sunch'ŏn, not marked in the manuscript)

54. What were our names, ages, and in what capacities we had sailed?

Hendrick Hamel, book-keeper	age 36
Govert Denijszen, quartermaster	age 47
Mattheus Eibocken, under surgeon	age 32
Jan Pieterszen, gunner	age 36
Gerrit Janszen, gunner	age 32
Cornelis Dirckse, junior boatswain	age 31
Benedictus Clercq, boy	age 27
Denijs Govertszen, boy	age 25

Thus asked and answered, this 14 September 1666.

Hamel's Journal

NOTES

1. This shows that the chief navigator, Hendrik Janse from Amsterdam, knew the existence of Quelpaert island. In a daily company register in Nagasaki, the island was mentioned in November 1647. Witsen writes: "Mattheus Eibokken, one of the survivors informed me that they had been captured on Quelpaert island, and that the chief navigator knew this island and had explained to them that now the Japanese have no authority there." (Witsen, 150). *Chejudo* stretches from 33 degrees 12 minutes to 33 degrees 30 minutes North latitude, which makes the observation of the chief navigator quite accurate, given the instruments of that time and the conditions of the place.

2. Hamel gives distances in 'mijlen'. Hoetink writes that these are the so called German miles, about 7.4 km to one 'mijl' which seamen used. There was however the English mile, about 1.6 km, the Dutch mile, about 5.8 km and similar measurements in other countries. The use of the Dutch word 'mijl' may avoid confusion.

3. Hamel does not mention the town of *Cheju*, but speaks about *Moggan* (*mok-kwan*), that is the residence of the *'Mocxa'* (*mok-sa*) the magistrate of the island (see also list of Korean words).

4. Hamel refers to the chief officials as 'governor', but *Chejudo* was under the administration of *Chŏlla* province (Ledyard, 147). "*Mok-sa*", Mandarin du 1er ordre dans les villes ou il y a des satellites pour arreter les voleurs (le 2e dans l'ordre civil, le 1er au-dessous du gouverneur)." (*Dictionaire Corean Francais*, 244)

5. "The most common drink, after what the clouds directly furnish, is the water in which rice has been boiled." (Griffis, *Corea*, 1905, 267)

6. *Kwanghaegun* was King *Hyojong's* great-uncle. He had reigned from 1608 to 1623, when he was dethroned. Exiled first to *Kangwha* island, he was later (1637) moved to *Cheju*, where he died in 1641. During his exile, there were attempts to restore him to the throne. (Ledyard, 25 & 148)

7. One catty (Malayan "kati") is about 600 grams.

8. The under-surgeon Mattheus Eibokken, from Enkhuizen, who must have been about 19 years old. (see interrogation in Nagasaki and numerous statements by Witsen)

9. In fact, Weltevree had been transferred to a Chinese junk that had been captured by the *Ouwerkerck*. Storms drove this junk close to the Korean coast where he and two companions were captured. (Ledyard, 36, and Hamel speaking to the Opperhoofd, the Company Director, in Deshima)

10. *'Benjoesen'* may be a corruption of the Japanese bungio or bugyo, meaning governor or superintendent. (C.J. Pernell, *The Logbook of William Adams*, 194)

11. Among the salvaged books was probably the logbook of the *Sperwer*. (*Hoetink*, 15)

12. Gerrit Jansz and Govert Denys, both from Rotterdam and Jan Pieters de Vries.

(*Hoetink*, 16)

13. This was a practice in China too, called the *'cangue'* by Europeans: "Public exposure in the *kia*, or cangue is considered rather a kind of censure or reprimand than a punishment, and carries no disgrace with it, nor comparatively much bodily suffering if the person be fed and screened from the sun. The frame weighs between twenty or thirty pounds, and is so made as to rest upon the shoulders without chafing the neck, but so broad as to prevent the person feeding himself. The name, residence, and offence of the delinquent are written upon it for the information of the passerby, and a policeman is stationed over him to prevent escape." (S. Wells Williams, *The Middle Kingdom*, 1890, 509)

14. "As Quelpaert has long been used as a place for banishment of convicts, the islanders are rude and unpolished.... Immense droves of horses and cattle are reared." (Griffis, *Corea*, 1905, 201)

15. *Ipamsansŏng* is a mountain fortress on *Naejangsan*, 763 m high. As a native of the Low Countries, Hamel may never before have crossed such a mountain pass.

16. The Dutchmen travelled about 30 km a day. The trip to *Seoul* took them at least 12 days. According to Korean sources they arrived in *Seoul* on 26 June 1654. (Ledyard, 51)

17. Hamel uses for 'seal' the Malayan word *tjap* used in the East Indies. These plaques were *ho-p'ae;* everyone in Korea had one. (Ledyard, 52)

18. This may be a misdescription as the tribute was brought to China and not collected: "The Coreans had a third of their tribute remitted in 1643 ... and in the following year, when sending home the king's son, who had gone to Peking to have his title to the crown confirmed, a half was remitted .... a yearly or half-yearly tribute is sent in to Peking, accompanied by a host of merchants, who bring back profits much greater than the amount of the tribute." (Ross, *History of Corea*, 288, 365)

19. Hamel does not state why he and his companions were sent away, but it was probably to conceal the fact that foreigners were drilling the royal troops. The suspicions of the new ruler at Peking were easily roused. (Griffis, *Corea*, 1905, 172)

20. *Namhansansŏng*, located about 25 km southeast of central *Seoul*, is a natural redoubt. Its steep sides shield it from approaching armies. It was constructed in 1621 by King *Kwanghaegun*. The Manchus laid siege to *Namhansansŏng* in the winter of 1635 and King Injo was forced to surrender and pledge his loyalty to the Manchu king.

21. A tael is a Chinese measure of weight, equivalent to 37.8 grams.

22. Near the *Hongje* bridge was a hostel at which the Manchu ambassador changed from his ceremonial uniform into his travelling clothes. (Ledyard, 135)

23. In the files of the military training bureau, the Korean names of the two are mentioned. Hendrik Janse was *Nam Puksan* and Hendrik Janse Bos was *Nam*

lan. (Ledyard, 60-61) This raises the question whether all Dutchmen were given the family name *Nam*?

24. "When the chief navigation officer, who was the leader of the Dutch captives, wanted to flee the country with the Manchu envoy, he was beheaded and they threatened to kill all the others." (Witsen, 50) It is strange that Weltevree could not, or did not want to tell anything about the fate of the prisoners. (*Hoetink,* 26) Korean sources say: "When the Ch'ing envoy came, one of them, *Nam Puksan,* laid his plaint directly before the envoy on the highway, begging to be returned to his country. The Ch'ing envoy was greatly alarmed and turned him over to this country to be held until further notice. But *Puksan,* nervous and sullen, starved himself to death. The court was very concerned over this, but the Ch'ing people never made any further inquiries." (Ledyard, 62)

25. Thus Hamel was not among those who spoke Korean well. (*Hoetink,* 26)

26. Possibly to use them on occasion as interpreters? (*Hoetink,* 26)

27. *Usuyŏng,* the "right naval garrison" about 30 km west of *Haenam.*

28. The Japanese compound at *Tongnae (Pusan).* "The possession of Fusan by the Japanese was, until 1876, a perpetual witness of the humiliating defeat of the Coreans in the war of 1592-1597, and a constant irritation to their national pride." (Griffis, *Corea,* 1905, 150)

29. The nineteenth king, *Hyojong,* commenced his political career at Moukden, where he had been sent as hostage by his father. In the second year of his reign, 1650, he organised the navy. He died in the year 1659. The twentieth king, *Hyonjong,* was born in Moukden, whence he returned a year before his father." (Parker, "Corea," *China Review* XIV, 63)

30. "Stores of rice are kept at certain places on the coast, in anticipation of dearth in adjoining provinces, and royal or local rewards are given to relief distributors according to merit." (Parker, "Corea," *China Review* XIV, 129)

31. Hamel does not mention *Yosu,* but *Saijsingh* and *Naijsingh.* He meant the Left Provincial Naval District, *Chawado Suyŏng (Chwasuyŏng),* located at *Naeyepo.* (Ledyard, 70) Until 1593 this had been the naval headquarters of Admiral *Yi Sun-shin,* Korea's most famous naval commander.

32. *Sunch'ŏn* was a provincial naval command post during the early Choson dynasty.

33. *Namwon* was once an administrative center of *Chŏllabukdo.* Remains of *Namwon* fortress are still visible.

34. Arriving in 1656 in *Chŏlla Pyŏngyŏng* they were 33. Seven years later they numbered 22; thus 11 men must have died.

35. A small island in front of *Yŏsu, Odongdo* is known for a special variety of bamboo, used for arrows by Korean archers of days past.

36. "Their boats are flat; in front as well as in the rear, they hang a little over the water. They use oars when sailing. They are not bulletproof. They dare not and may not, except with special permission, go far out of sight from the land,

for which they are unfit. Their construction is exceedingly light. One sees hardly any iron; wooden pegs are used. Anchors are of wood. They sail as far as China." (Witsen, 56) "The Coreans are not a seafaring people. They do not sail out from land, except upon rare occasions. The prow and stern of fishing-boats are much alike, and are neatly nailed together with wooden nails. They use round stems of trees in their natural state, for masts. The sails are made of straw, plaited together with cross-bars of bamboo. The sail is at the stern of the boat. They sail very well within three points of the wind, and the fisher-men are very skilful in managing them." (Griffis, *Corea*, 1905, 195) "Although Koreans seldom sail to Japan, they know where it is, and on what point it is distanced, without that knowledge which the Dutchmen overheard, they never would have been able to escape to Japan, since they had no map and nobody among them had ever been there." (Witsen, 44)

37. "A large comet was seen on 27 November 1664 until after New Year 1665." (*Hollandse Mercurius* XV, 1665, 183)

38. See *Diary of Richard Cocks* II, 7 November–23 December 1618, 93-105.

39. "The people in this place (*Firando*) did talke much about this comett seene, that it did prognosticate some great matter of warr, and whether I knew what it did meane or would ensue thereof; unto which I answerd that such many tymes have byn seene in our partes of the world, but the meaning therof God did know and not I." (*Diary of Richard Cocks* II, November 1618, 94-98)

40. "*Yi Tobin*, the former Naval Commandant of the Left District of *Cholla* Province, did not violate the regulations in the slightest. He was very consci-entious in carrying out his duties, keeping in repair all the official buildings, walls, fortifications, ships and military equipment. He was especially con-cerned to treat his men with love and kindness. He set up a bondloosening office. He was generous in providing grain and cloth to cover the livery expenses incurred in welcoming and sending off his junior officers. The local militia and the regular soldiers attached to the garrison under his command praise him to this day: 25 December 1666." (Ledyard, 72)

41. "Gunpowder and printing has been known to them for 1000 years, they say, as well as the compass, although it looks different than in our country. They use but a small piece of wood, sharp in front and obtuse in the back. They throw this in a bucket of water and the sharp point indicates the North. The magnetic force must be in it. They know 8 points of the compass, there are also com-passes of two pieces of wood, put crosswise, one point sticking out points to the North." (Witsen, 56)

42. "North and West winds prevail in winter, South and East winds in summer. North-East monsoon is inapplicable to the coasts of Japan and their vicinity, with the exception of the southerly islands." (Rein, "The Climate of Japan," *Transactions of the Asiatic Society of Japan,* Vol. VI, 1878, 507 & 509)

43. The real distance is about 210 km.

VOC ships leaving Holland for the Indies.
by Willem van de Velde, 1649, National Maritime Museum, Greenwich

The 8 original illustrations on woodblock, Stichter edition, Rotterdam 1668

20.   J O U R N A E L.

wp van baen quamen / en dat wp over lange jaren ons schip verlooren hadden / ende ne-
sochten na nangesackp te gaen / om weder bp ons volck te komen / waren doe wat beter
te gemoet / doch niet sonder vreese / door dien de Coereepers ons wijs gemaeckt hadden /
dat al de vreemde natie die op de Japanse Cust komen te vervallen / door geslagen wierden. Den 9 ditto bewaerdense ons in 't vaartupgh / als mede de twee die aen landt / des-
gelijcks mede den 10 ende den 11 ditto / versagen ons van toespijs / water / brant / hout /
ende 't gene meer van nooden was / deckten 't vaartupgh door dient gestadigh regende /
met stroope matjes. Den 12 ditto versagen ons van alles wat op de reps na nangesackp
noodigh was: lichten 't ancker / ende quamen dien avont aen de binnexp van 't Eplant-
voor een dorp ten ancker / alwaer wp dien nacht bleven leggen. Den 13 ditto met Zonne
opganck gingh de voorsz. derde persoon in een barck / bp hem hebbende eenige goederen
en brieven / die aen 't Kepsers-hof moesten wesen / lichten ons ancker / met ons bp hebbende 2 kleyne ende groote barcken : de twee aen landt gebrochte maets / waren in een
van de groote barcken / ende quamen op nangesackn eerst weder bp ons: in den avont

quamen wp
in de bay / en
de des Mid-
dernachts op
de reede van
Nange sackp
ten ancker /
sagen daer 5
Hollantsche
Schepen leg-
gen / gelijck
ons te voo-
ren gewesen
worden : des
Morghens
den 14. ditto
wierden wp
aen landt ge-
bracht / ende
van des Ed.
Compagnie-
ens Colck

verwellekomt / die ons alles ondervraeght hebbende / prees ons seer / dat wp met soo
een kleyn oudt vaartupgh / onse drpheyt over. soo een wydt vaarwater gesocht ende ghe-
kregen hadden / belastende de Colck / ons op 't Eplandt ofte in Compagnies Logie te
brengen : daer komende wierden van de Ed. Heer Willem Volgers Opperhoost / Sr.
Nicolaes de Rop tweede persoon / ende sijn Ed. voordre bp hebbende suppoosten wel ont-
haelt / ende op onse manier weder in de kleederen gesteecken / waer voor haer de Almo-
gende tot danckbaerheyt / sijn geluckigen zegen ende langhduerende gesontheyt belieft te
geven : wp konnen den goeden Godt niet genoech bedancken / dat hp ons upt soo een ghe-
vangenisse / soo veel droefheyt en perijckel van 13 jaren 28 dagen / soo genadelijck verlost
heeft / verhopende dat de andere 8 aldaer gebleven Maets / mede soodanige verlossinge
mogen erlangen / en oock weder bp onse Natie geraken / waer toe haer den Almogenden
behulpsaem sal belieben te zijn / Amen.

End of the Journal, Stichter edition, Rotterdam, 1668

BESCHRYVINGE

Van't Koninghrijck

COEREE,

Met alle hare Kechten, Ordon-
nantien, ende Maximen, foo inde Politie, als
inde Melitie, als vooren verhaelt.

ANNO M.DC.LXVIIJ.

Frontispiece of the "Description", Stichter edition, Rotterdam 1668

A DESCRIPTION
OF THE KINGDOM OF KOREA

Geographical Situation

The country we call Korea is called *Chosŏn-kuk* by the inhabitants. It is situated between 34 1/2 and 44 degrees North latitude and is from South to North about 140-150 mijl long, and from East to West about 70 to 75 mijl wide. Korean cartographers represent the country as an oblong rectangle, like a playing card, although there are several points reaching out into the sea.

The country is divided into 8 provinces, in which one finds 360 towns and furthermore a great number of forts and castles, partly situated in the mountains and partly along the coasts. To approach the country by ship is very perilous for anyone who does not know the coastline, for there are many reefs and mudshoals impeding a safe passage.

The country is densely populated[1] and in favourable years is able to provide amply for all its own needs because of the abundance of rice, cereals and cotton growing in the southern half of the country. To the southeast, the country is very close to Japan. The distance between the city of *Pusan* and the city of *Osaka*[2] is only 25 to 26 mijl. In the strait between them is the island of *Tsushima*, called *Taemado* by the Koreans. According to the Koreans this island used to be Korean, but in the war with Japan it was by agreement exchanged for Quelpaert (*Chejudo*).

On the West the kingdom is separated from China by the Bay of Nanking. In the North the country is linked to one of the Northernmost provinces of China by a great high mountain, so that it is not completely an island.[3]

Fishery

To the Northeast lies a vast sea. There one finds every year some whales with Dutch harpoons, as well as of other nations, embedded in them.[4] In the months of December, January, February and March herring is caught in large quantities. During the first two months the herring are like the kind we catch in the North Sea. After that a smaller kind is caught, like the frying herring in our country.[5] Thus a passage must exist leading from Waeijgat[6] to Korea and Japan. We often asked Korean navigators if, while sailing in the Northeastern seas, there was any land there. To which they answered that nothing but open seas lay in that direction.

Climate and Agriculture

Travellers from Korea to China nearly always go by ship through the narrowest part of the Bay, because in winter the mountains are bitterly cold and in summer a passage overland is dangerous, because of the wild animals. Some winters the rivers are frozen. One can travel easily over the ice. It freezes hard and much snow falls, as we saw in the year 1662 when we were in a monastery in the mountains. Houses and trees were snowed under so that tunnels had been dug to go from one house to the other. In order to move around, Koreans put small planks under their feet with which they know how to climb, or walk down and not sink in the snow.

In the north people live on barley and millet, because rice cannot grow there. Cotton does not grow there either, and so it must be transported from the south. Common people in these regions eat poorly and mostly are miserably clad in hemp, in linen, or in hides. But in these regions grows the ginseng plant.[7] The root of this plant is used to pay tribute to the Chinese and much is exported to China and Japan.

Monarchy[8]

As concerns the authority of the King, he is sovereign in Korea, although he is a vassal of the Tartar.[9] He exercises unlimited authority, without obeying his crown council. There are no feudal lords in the country possessing towns, villages, or islands. The important men take their income from landed property and slaves. Some of them possess no less than 2,000 to 3,000 slaves. Also there are those who receive from the crown the loan of some islands, or estates, but as soon as they die these lapse and return to the King.

The Army

To defend the country there are several thousand troops in the royal city, cavalry as well as foot soldiers. They are maintained by the King. Their task is to guard the court and to protect the King when he travels.

Each province is obliged once every 7 years in rotation, to send to the royal city some free men, to protect the palace of the King; each year from a different province. Each province has a general who has 3 or 4 colonels under him. Under every colonel stands a number of captains, each of whom is commandant of a town.

Every quarter in a city has a sergeant, every village a corporal and at the head of each group of 10 men stands a leader. All officers and non-commissioned officers have to keep lists on which all ratings under their command are recorded. These lists have to be handed over to the superiors. In this way the King knows at all times precisely how many soldiers he can muster.

Horsemen wear armour and helmet. As weapons they carry swords, bow and arrow, and a sort of flail with short iron points, like we use in our fatherland for threshing grain. Some soldiers wear armour and helmets fashioned of iron plates and horn. They are armed with muskets, swords and shortpikes.[10] The officers are armed with bow and arrow. Every soldier must carry with him, and pay for out of his own expenses, gunpowder and bullets for 50 shots. [When we served in Seoul we once received 5 strokes on our bare buttocks because we had not enough gun-powder with us. (*Stichter* edition)]

Every town has to appoint in turns a number of monks from the surrounding monasteries for the maintenance of the fortresses and fortifications in the mountains, at their own expense. In time of need these monks are used as soldiers. They are armed with swords, and with bow and arrow. They are considered the best soldiers of the country.[11] They are under the command of a captain chosen from among their own ranks. They too are marked on the lists, so that the King at all times knows how many free men, be it soldiers, officers, workers or monks, are in his service for the country. Those who have reached the age of sixty are discharged from military service. Their place is taken by their children.

Noblemen who are not in the royal service, or who have been discharged from service, together with slaves, only have to pay royal, or country tax. They amount to more than half of the population, because if a free man begets a child by a female slave, or a slave begets a child by a free woman, the offspring in either case will be a slave. Children born from slaves become the property of the female slave.

The Navy

Every town must maintain a war junk, with crew, ammunition and other accessories. These junks have two decks and 20 to 24 oars. At each oar sit 5 or 6 oarsmen. The total crew consists of 200 to 300 men, soldiers and oarsmen. The junks are equipped with countless small pieces and a quantity of firearms (10 a).

Each province has an admiral who drills the crews of the junks and inspects these every year. He reports his findings to the admiral general, who on occasion personally reviews naval exercises. If the admiral or the captains ascertain the slightest shortcomings in the discharge of duties, the culprits will be exiled or banned, or condemned to death, as happened with our admiral in 1666.

The Government

The state council, consisting of high and low ranking officers, serves as an advisory council to the King. Daily they gather in the palace, presenting all events to the King. They may not oblige the King to do anything, but assist him by word and deed. Besides the King they are the most prominent people in the country. As long as they do not misbehave, they remain members of the council until their eightieth year. This applies to all officials in the service of the King, unless they are demoted.

The term of office of a city governor (*stadhouder*) is one year. Other civil servants, officials of both high and low ranks, serve three years, though many are relieved of their posts before their term of office expires, due to some misstep they have committed. The King always has his spies at large to procure good information about everything concerning the government. Many an official risks death or lifelong exile.

Revenues

Concerning the revenues of the King, the landlords, towns and villages, the King derives his income from taxes levied on production of agriculture and fisheries. In every town, or village, he has warehouses to store the crops, or his revenue. He lends out to commoners at an interest rate of 10%, collected upon harvesting of the crops.

The landlords live off their own income, and those who are in the service of the King live off the stipends they receive from him. City authorities also levy taxes on the land area on which houses are built, in towns as well as in the countryside. The level of the imposition depends on the area of the land. The proceeds are used to pay the magistrates and servants of the King, as well as for the maintenance of local provisions.

Anyone who has not fulfilled his military service must instead render labor service during 3 months per year, in the course of which he will be called upon to perform all kinds of tasks necessary for maintenance of the land.

Horsemen and soldiers in towns and villages have to hand over every year 3 pieces of linen, or the equivalent in silver, for the maintenance of hired horsemen and soldiers. Other taxes or duties do not exist in this country.

Justice

High treason and other serious criminal offences against the King, or the state, are very harshly punished. The entire family of the culprit is destroyed. His house is razed to the ground and on that site never again may a proper house be constructed. All his goods and his slaves are confiscated. They are either used in the service of the country, or given away to others.

If someone finds fault with a sentence pronounced by the King, or on his behalf, he will be put to death. In our time it happened that the sister-in-law of the King was very skillful with the needle. The King ordered her to make a robe for him. It so happened that this woman despised the King, so she sewed some magical herbs in the lining of the robe, so that whenever the King wore it he could find no rest. The King ordered the stitches to be pulled out and the garment to be inspected. The evil stuff hidden inside was discovered. He had the lady confined in a room with a floor of copper plates under which a fire was lit until she died. An acquaintance of this lady, at that moment a high ranking official of noble birth, highly respected at the court, protested. He wrote to the King that a woman, and moreover a lady of distinguished position, could have been punished in another way. The King summoned the high official. He received in one day 120 strokes on his shins and was then beheaded. All his goods and slaves were confiscated. Such an offence, and other offences to be mentioned later, are deemed personal offences; the family of the culprit is not also punished, as occurs in cases of high treason.

A woman who kills her husband is buried up to her shoulders along a highway over which many pass. Beside her is placed a wooden saw with which all passers-by, except nobility, must saw once at the head until she dies. The town in or near which the murder occurred, loses for some years the right to have its own commander. During such a period the town is ruled by the commander of a nearby town, or by a nobleman. The same penalty is applied if someone complains about his magistrate, and the court finds him in the wrong. A man who kills his wife goes free if he can prove he had any reason, such as adultery or the like. A man who slays a female slave has to pay the master of the slave threefold her worth. Slaves who kill their masters are tortured to death. A master may kill his slave for a minor offense. Murderers are killed in the same way as they killed their victims, but first several lashes are administered to the soles of their feet. Anyone who is guilty of murder is punished as follows: the corpse of the victim is washed all over with vinegar and dirty, stinking water. This mixture is poured through a funnel into the mouth of the criminal until his body is full, then they beat his swollen belly until it bursts.

Theft and burglary are severely punished, but there still is much stealing. Thieves generally are beaten on their footsoles until slowly they die. Anyone who commits adultery with or abducts a married woman is led through the town together with that woman, sometimes naked, or clad in thin drawers, faces covered with lime. An arrow is pierced through both their ears. Behind them a small drum is tied on which a servant of the law beats, crying: "They are adulterers!". Having been led thus through the town they receive 50 or 60 blows each on the buttocks.

Anyone who fails to pay the King's tax on time is beaten twice or thrice a month on the shinbones, until he pays the delinquent sum, or else dies. If he dies his relatives have to settle the debt, thus the King of this country never misses his income.

The standard punishment consists of flogging on the naked buttocks, or on the calves. This is considered no shame, for even a lightly spoken word can lead to such punishment.

An ordinary magistrate may not condemn someone to death, without the concurrence of the provincial governor. Crimes concerning the state cannot be prosecuted without informing the King.

Beatings on the shins happen as follows : the condemned is seated on a stool with his legs bound together. On his shins they put two stripes, one about the width of a hand above the feet, and likewise under the knees. In between he is struck with a wooden rod as long as an arm, made of oak or ash, two fingers wide in front, thick as a one crown piece, and rounded behind. After more than 30 blows the condemned is given a rest of 3 or 4 hours, after which the punishment continues until justice is achieved. Those they intend to kill are beaten with heavier sticks 3 to 4 feet long, as wide as an arm, and the beating is done directly under the knees.

Beatings to the bottoms of the feet are done as follows: the condemned is seated on the ground, the great toes are bound together and a piece of wood is placed between the thighs. With round sticks as wide as an arm he receives as many blows on the soles of his feet as the judge pleases. This is also the method by which all criminals are tortured.

Beatings on the buttocks happen as follows: the condemned must lower his trousers and lie prostrate on the floor, or sometimes bend over a bench to which he is tied down. Out of moral consideration women may keep on small pants that are wetted so as to be better hit. Flat boards four or five feet long are used, rounded above, as wide as a hand and thick as a little finger. One hundred strokes brings death. Beating also is done with rods or bundles of switches, thick as fingers and 2 to 3 feet long, with the man or woman standing on a little bench. This happens with so much wailing of bystanders that the noise is more frightening than the beating. Children are punished with strokes of smaller switches on their calves. There are still other punishments, but to relate them here would take too long.

Religion

As regards their religion, temples, monks and religious groups, the ordinary people do pay their idols some superstitious rites, but they have more respect for the public authority than for their many gods. The higher ranks and nobility do not show any respect for idols. They seem to esteem themselves higher than the idols.

When someone, whether of high rank or low, dies, monks come to say prayers and to bring offerings for the deceased whose family and friends are present. When a person of high rank dies, relatives and friends, sometimes from 30-40 mijl away, assemble to attend the ceremonies to honour the memory of the deceased.

On all feast days civilians and farmers come to honour the idols. They put a stick of sweet-smelling wood in a small pot in front of the statues as a burnt offering. And when they have paid reverence they simply depart again. They claim that one who does good will receive a reward in the hereafter and one who does evil will be punished for that.

Preaching and catechism are unknown to them, neither do they instruct one another in their faith. Even if they have any faith, they never debate about religion. All through the country idols are venerated in the same fashion.

Twice a day a monk prays before the statues, during which he makes an offering. On feast days many people come to the temples and all the monks raise a clamor, clashing cymbals, beating drums and playing other instruments.

There is a multitude of monasteries and temples in the country, all beautifully situated in the mountains. Each one is under the jurisdiction of some town. In some monasteries live as many as 500 or 600 monks, and some towns have 3,000 or 4,000 monks under their jurisdiction. They live in houses in which 10, 20 or 30 monks are staying, sometimes less, or more. In each dwelling the eldest monk has the leadership. If one of the monks is misbehaving the leader can administer 20 or 30 strokes to his buttocks. But for a serious offence a monk is turned over to the magistrate of the local town. There is no lack of monks, if only their doctrine were good. Anyone who so wishes can become a monk and then quit if it does not suit him. The monks are not highly esteemed in this country. They are counted little better than country slaves, because of the high tribute they must pay and the base work they are obliged to do.

The high ranking monks are much esteemed, however, mainly because of their erudition. They are considered to belong to the scholars of the country. They are known as the King's monks. They carry the state seal and exercise a magistrate's jurisdiction when they visit the

monasteries. They travel on horseback and are received with much ceremonial honour.

Monks may not eat animal flesh or anything from which a living
thing comes. They do not eat eggs. Their heads and chins are clean
shaven. They may not converse with women. Transgressors of these
rules receive 70 or 80 blows on the buttocks and are banished from the
monastery. On entering a monastery, after their tonsure, young monks
receive a brand on one arm,[12] so that one always can see that they have
been a monk. Ordinary monks have to scrape for their food through toil,
trade and begging.

In every monastery one finds a number of small boys whom the
monks diligently instruct so that they become good readers and writers.
When these boys begin to shave they become the servants of their
instructors. All they earn is for these monks, until he sets them free. If
these monks die, they become their heirs and wear mourning. Those
who are emancipated observe mourning as well, out of gratitude for
those who brought them up and instructed them as a father would have
done for his child.

There are still others, who like monks render devotions to the idols
and abstain from meat, but they do not shave their heads and they may
marry.[13]

Monasteries and temples are built with donations collected from ordinary people as well as wealthy notables, everyone contributing according to capability. The monks work and in exchange receive food and
some allowance given by the monk in charge, appointed by the magistrate of the town with jurisdiction over the monastery.

Many monks believe that long ago all people spoke the same language, but when people built a tower in order to climb into heaven the
whole world changed.

Noblemen often go to a monastery to enjoy themselves with whores
and other company, because the monasteries are very beautifully situated in the mountains amidst woods. They are counted as the best houses
in the country, but they should be considered brothels and taverns rather
than temples. One should know that in the ordinary monasteries the
monks are much inclined to drinking.

Near us in the royal city were two nunneries, one for noble women and one for ordinary women. They too had their hair shaven, and they ate and worshipped in the same way as the monks. They were living on an allowance from the King and the nobles. Four or five years ago the present King[14] abolished both nunneries and gave the nuns permission to marry.[15]

Housing

As concerns houses and furniture, among the well-to-do one finds many beautiful homes, but the common people must make do with mean dwellings. They are not permitted to make any improvements to their homes. Nobody may cover his house with a roof of tiles without consent of the magistrate. Most houses are shingled or thatched with reeds or straw. The yards are separated from one another by a wall or a fence. The houses stand on wooden pillars. The lower part of the walls is of stone. Above this small timber is tied crosswise. The outside and inside are smoothed out with clay and sand. On the inside the walls are covered with white paper. During the winter, a fire is lit every day under the floors, so that the rooms are always warm, more like an oven than a room (15 a). The floors are covered with oiled paper. The houses have but one story, above which is a little loft where some small things can be stored.

Noblemen always have in front of the house properly speaking a separate house where they receive family and friends, who sometimes stay overnight. They use this separate living accommodation also to relax and to rest. In general this space offers a view over a large inner court with a pond and a garden, decorated with many flowers and other rare plants, trees and rocks. Women live in the rear part of the house, so that they cannot be stared at by every passer by.

Merchants and notables have next to their houses a warehouse in which they can store goods, keep office and receive their relations, whom they usually treat to tobacco and liquor. Married women are free to visit everyone, but at banquets they sit together, opposite their husbands.

In general homes are scarcely furnished, there are but the daily necessities. There are many taverns and pleasure houses, where men go to hear and see whores dance, sing and play musical instruments. In summertime Koreans go to the mountains to relax in the woods.

Travelling and Hospitality

Inns in which travellers can stay overnight are unknown. Those travelling along the road, towards evening enter the inner court of any private house, if it is not a nobleman's, where they unpack as much rice as they want to eat, which the host at once has cooked and served with side dishes to his guests. In many villages households take turns without murmuring.[16]

Along the highway to Seoul are real stopping places, where travellers, officials and common people alike, can stay overnight. Nobility and those coming from the countryside, travelling along other roads, rest overnight at the homes of local magistrates along the way, where they receive food as well.

Marriage

Relatives within the fourth degree are not allowed to marry one another. Courtship does not exist, for marriages are contracted by the parents when the children are only 8, 10 or 12 years old. In general the girls go to live in the house of the parents of the boy, unless her own parents have no sons. They remain there until they have learned how to manage a house and how to make a living. Before the marriage the bridegroom makes a tour of the town accompanied by relatives and friends. The bride is accompanied by her parents and family to the new house of the bridegroom. There the wedding is celebrated without any further ceremony.

A man may dismiss his wife even if he has already begot several children with her. Then he can take another wife. A woman has no such privilege, unless a judge has granted it to her. A man may have as many wives as he can support and feed. If he likes he goes to whorehouses, without being condemned. Only one wife stays in his house and runs the household. The other women live elsewhere in separate houses. Nobility in general have two or three women in their home, one of whom is in control over the household. Each of these women has her own apartment where the master of the house visits as he pleases.

This nation treats their women as no more than female slaves, whom they can renounce on account of a trifle. If the man does not want the children, the renounced woman must take them all with her. Little wonder this country is so densely populated.

Education

The nobility and well-to-do people give their children a good education. They take tutors in their service to teach them how to read and write, skills to which this nation is much inclined. This is done gently and with good manners. The children are constantly being told about the many wise sages of the past and how these obtained rank and honour. They mostly sit day and night and read. It is admirable to see how these young boys know and explain the texts which form the basis of their learning.

In every town is a building where those who have given their life for the fatherland are commemorated each year. In these places old writings worthy of preservation are housed. Noblemen practice reading there.

Every year in each province, examination sessions are held in two or three towns. Examiners visit to test the knowledge of those seeking employment in the military and the police as well. The names of those who are found fit to be vested with executive powers are passed on to the court. There every year a session is held, where candidates from across the entire country are examined by the King's delegates. All the important people of the country gather there, those who formerly served in government posts, those who are in service, as well as those seeking promotions in the police and the military.

Those who pass the examination receive a letter of promotion from the King. This is a much coveted document. Graduation has made many a young nobleman an aged beggar, because he may exhaust his means of subsistence — often but modest — in the high expenses of donations and banquets he is expected to give. Many parents invest large sums for the study of their children. Not a few never succeed in actually obtaining the government post which was their goal. But the bare fact that their sons are promoted in name, offers satisfaction to parents and compensates for their sacrifices.

Parents love their children very much, as do children their parents. If parents have committed a crime from which they escaped, the children have to answer for it, as parents for their children.

Slave parents have little regard for their children, because they know that the owners will take their children away from them as soon as they are able to work.

Mourning

For a deceased father all children mourn for three years, and for a deceased mother, two years. During that period the children eat the same food as monks and they are not allowed to hold any employment. Anyone who has lost a parent yet who holds a function, important or of no importance, must immediately resign his office. During mourning sexual intercourse with their wives is forbidden. Children conceived during that period are considered to be bastards. During that period they may not quarrel or fight, nor indulge in liquor. They wear long robes of raw hemp with no hem below, and no hat. As a girdle they use a string of hemp as thick as a shipscable or the arm of grown man. Around their head they wear a cord, a little thinner, with a bamboo hat. In their hand they carry a thick stick, or a bamboo staff, so that one can see whether someone mourns his father or his mother. The bamboo signifies the father, while the stick shows that the mother has died. Mourners wash or clean themselves very little, so they look more like scarecrows than humans.

When someone has died his relatives act as if they are mad. They weep and scream along the streets, pulling their hair from their head.

Special attention is given to burial. Fortune-tellers fix a suitable burial place, mostly in the mountains where floods cannot reach. The dead body is laid in a double coffin, each layer 2 inches thick. New clothes and other goods according to the wealth of the deceased are put in the coffins. Interment normally is done in springtime or autumn, after the rice is harvested. Those who die in summertime are provisionally entombed in a small straw hut erected on poles. At the time of the funeral the coffin is brought back to the house where the body is put in a coffin with clothes and goods as mentioned above. They carry the coffin away in the early morning, after having made merry all through the night. The bearers do nothing but dance and sing, while the relatives follow the body weeping and wailing. On the third day, family and friends return again to the tomb to bring offerings, making a joyful outing of it.

In general tombs are topped with a small mound of earth, 4, 5 or 6 feet high, very neatly arranged. Prominent people are entombed after death in graves with standing stones and carved statues. On the stones are cut the dead man's name, his descent and the position he held. On the 15th day of the 8th month the grass on the tomb is cut and new rice is offered. Next to New Year this is the most important feast day of the year. Their calendar is based on the cycles of the moon, thus after 3 years of 12 months there is a year with 13 months.

There are fortune tellers and sorceresses. They do nobody any harm. They ascertain whether the deceased died quietly, or restless, and whether he is buried in the right spot. If according to them this is not the case, the body is exhumed and reburied elsewhere. Sometimes it happens that tombs are relocated 3 or more times.

After the funeral rites for the parents are finished the eldest son remains in the ancestral home and keeps all that belongs to it. The other possessions, landed property and goods are divided among the other sons. We have never heard that daughters inherit anything (if there are sons), nor do wives, who keep only their clothes and what belonged to her and was brought in at her wedding.

If the parents reach eighty years old they have to hand their property over to the eldest son, for they are considered incapable of managing anything anymore. But they remain highly respected. On his own property the son builds a house for his parents to live in and cares for them.[17]

Character

As concerns loyalty and disloyalty, as well as courage, this nation is much inclined to stealing, lying and cheating. One should not trust them too much. They consider it an act of heroism when they have cheated someone; it is not considered a shame. When someone has been duped by a merchant in the purchase of horses or cows it can be cancelled even after 3 or 4 months. Dealings in land and realty can be cancelled as long as payment has not been made.

On the other hand Koreans are good natured and very credulous. We could make them believe anything we wanted. They like strangers, especially the monks. They have a feminine sensitivity; reliable people told us how a number of years ago, when their King was murdered by the Japanese, they burned down and destroyed towns and villages. The Dutchman Jan Janse Weltevree told us that when the Tartar came over the ice and occupied the country more soldiers hanged themselves in the woods, than were killed by the enemy. They do not consider committing suicide to be shameful, they pity such people, saying they did it out of necessity (17a).

It also happened that some Dutch, English or Portuguese ships on their way to Japan were blown off course into Korean coastal waters and when Korean war junks tried to seize these ships, the crews fouled their pants and returned with nothing achieved.

They abhor blood. As soon as some fall in combat the rest flee. They have a great aversion to illnesses, especially contagious maladies. In that case at once they carry the sick person from his house outside the town, or village, where he lives and bring him to a small thatched hut out in the fields, made for that purpose. There nobody approaches him, or speaks to him, but those who look after him. Those who pass by spit on the ground in front of the sick. Those without friends to help them perish without being looked after.

In case of an epidemic access to the houses or the village is barred with branches of pinewood and the roofs of the houses of the stricken are covered with thornbrambles so that everyone will know.

Trade

Concerning trade with foreign countries as well as among themselves, the only people who do business here are the Japanese from the island of *Tsushima*, who have a trading post on the Southeast side of the city of *Pusan,* belonging to the lord of that island.

The Japanese export pepper, sappan-wood, alum, buffalohorn, deer- and buckskin and other merchandise they import from us and the Chinese and exchange for other Korean goods, to be processed in Japan. There is some trade with Peking and the North of China. Korean merchants travel on horseback overland to China and thus it is very costly, only the wealthy merchants can do it. Those who travel from the royal city (*Seoul*) to Peking and back are at least three months on the way.

Interior trade uses as means of exchange mostly pieces of linen.[18] The important businessmen and merchants use silver, but farmers and ordinary people use rice and other cereals.

Before the Tartar seized control of Korea this was a country of abundance and playfulness. People did nothing but eat, drink and be merry. But now they have suffered so much from the Tartars and the Japanese that in bad years they hardly have enough to keep going, because of the heavy tributes they have to provide, mainly to the Tartar, who comes three times per year to collect these.[19]

The Surrounding World

Koreans think there are but twelve countries or kingdoms in the whole world. They claim that once these countries were all subject to the emperor of China and that they had to pay tribute to him. Meanwhile all are thought to have liberated themselves since the Tartar took possession of China but could not conquer the other countries. They call the Tartar *Taekuksa* and *Orangkai* (Barbarian). They call our country *Namban-kuk*, which is what the Japanese used to call Portugal. About us, or about Holland, they know nothing. They got the name *Namban-kuk* from the Japanese and this name is renowned among them because of tobacco. Fifty or sixty years ago they knew nothing of tobacco. Then the Japanese taught them how to grow tobacco and how to use it. The seeds, according to the Japanese, came from *Namban-kuk* and so it is still often called *nambankoy*. It is now in wide use, not only among men but even by children 4 or 5 years old, as well as among women. One finds few people who do not smoke at all. When tobacco was first introduced they gave for each pipe a measure of silver (about 4 grams), or its equivalent. *Namban-kuk* therefore is one of the best known countries.

In their old writings it is written that there are 84,000 countries in the world, but they consider this a fiction, saying one ought to count islands, cliffs and rocks among them, for the sun could never in one day shine on so many countries at once. When we mentioned a number of countries they all laughed at us, saying these must be names of cities and villages, because their maps do not reach beyond Siam.

Farming and Mining

This country can be self-sufficient for the needs of the people. There is an abundance of rice and other cereals. They weave cotton and hemp. There are also many silkworms, but they have insufficient knowledge of spinning silk to weave material of good quality.

There is mining of silver, iron and lead[20], and trade in tigerskin and ginseng roots and other products.

Medicine

They grow plenty of medicinal herbs, but the ordinary people have little need of them, for they cannot afford doctors, who all are in the service of important people. Korea is by nature a very healthy country.[21]

Common people use the blind and fortune-tellers as doctors. They heed their counsel, either in making offerings in the mountains, near rivers, on cliffs or rocks, or in idol sanctuaries to call upon the devil, but this is not done anymore since these were abolished and destroyed at the King's command in 1662.

Weights, Measures and Money

Measures, ells and weights as far as the state and the merchants are concerned are equal throughout the country, but among the common people and the small hawkers much cheating goes on. Buyers often encounter shortages by weight or count, while sellers scales read too heavy.

Although in most provinces governors exercise good supervision they are unable to stamp out abuses, for everybody uses their own measures and weights.

They know no other money than the *Cash*, which is only current at the border with China. Silver is paid by weight in larger and smaller pieces, like the tael of silver in Japan.

Fauna

There are the following animals and birds. There are many horses,[22] cows, and bulls, which seldom are castrated. The farmers use cows and bulls to plough the land. Travellers and merchants use horses to transport goods. There are many tigers as well. Tigerskin is exported to China and Japan. There are bears, deer, wild boar and tame pigs, dogs, foxes, cats and the like. There are many snakes and venomous animals.

There are swans, geese, ducks, fowl, storks, herons, cranes, eagles, falcons, magpies, crows, cuckoos, pigeons, woodcocks, pheasants, skylarks, finches, thrushes, pewits and buzzards, and many other kinds of birds, and all in abundance.

Writing and Printing

As far as language, writing and calculation are concerned, the Korean speech is different from all other tongues. It is very difficult to learn because they have different names to express the same thing. They speak very fast or slow, especially among important people and scholars.

They write in three different ways. The first way, or the main one, is like the Chinese and the Japanese. In that way all their books are printed as well as official state records concerning the government. The second way is very fast, like the current writing in the fatherland. This way is much used by important people and governors when they write judgements or add a recommendation to requests, as well as in writing letters to one another. Common people cannot read this script very well. The third way is used by women and common people. It is very easy to learn and one is able to write everything. One can write down names one has never heard before, easier and better than in the other ways. All this is done with pencils, very skillfully and quickly. [23]

They have many manuscripts and printed books from olden times. They esteem these very highly, as shown by the fact that the brother of the king, or the prince of the realm, always has the superintendence of these books.

Copies and printing blocks are kept in safety in many cities, so that in case of fire, or otherwise, knowledge does not get lost. Their almanacs and the like are printed in China, since they lack the knowledge to do this in Korea. They print with wooden blocks, each side of the paper has its own special block.

Arithmetic and Bookkeeping

They calculate with long sticks, like the counters in our fatherland. They have no knowledge of mercantile bookkeeping: when they buy something they note down purchase price and then they note again the price of sale, subtract and see what remains or how much is short.

Royal Processions[24]

When the King rides out of his palace he is attended by all the nobility (dressed in black silk robes on which a coat of arms or some other
emblem is embroidered front and back, and a large broad girdle is worn
over it). Horsemen and footmen who receive the King's ration are in
front, each one wearing his best attire, with lots of flags and music,
played on all kinds of instruments. They are followed by the King's ret-
inue, made up of the most prominent citizens of the city. In the middle
of them sits the King in a palanquin, in the form of a beautifully gilded
small house. It grows so silent that one can hear the hush of the people
and the trampling of the horses. Just in front of the King rides the secretary, or another servant of His Majesty, with a small closed box into
which the subjects can place petitions to the King, either because they
have been wronged by the government, or by someone else, or are persons who cannot get any judgement from a judge, or whose parents or
friends are being punished unjustly, and any other kind of appeal. These
petitions are tied to a bamboostick, or hung on a wall, or handed over
from behind a fence, then picked up by servants who put them in the
box. When the King returns home the box is delivered to him and all
the petitions are put at the disposal of his Majesty. Then the King
pronounces his final verdicts, which are executed at once without
contradiction.[25]

Every street through which the King passes is closed off on both
sides. Nobody may open any door, or window, or leave it open, much
less look over the wall, or fence. When the King passes in front of the
nobility and military one has to turn his back, without looking back or
coughing. Therefore most soldiers put a small wooden stick in their
mouth, like the bit of a horse.

Visits of Chinese Envoys

When a Chinese envoy arrives, the King in person, together with all
the prominent officials, has to greet him outside the city and make a

deep bow to pay reverence. They all then escort him to his residence. He is shown more deference on his arrival and departure than the King. He is preceded by musicians, dancers and acrobats, showing their arts on the way. Also many treasures made and created in Korea are borne before him.

During a Chinese envoy's stay in the royal city the streets leading from his residence to the royal court are closed off by soldiers, who stand about 17 to 20 meters apart. Two or three do nothing else but bring notes out of the Chinese residence to the court, so that the King from moment to moment knows how the ambassador is doing. In fact they look for every means to honour him and receive him well, out of respect for his lord, and to keep the envoy from making complaints about them.

*   *   *

Conclusion

To visit the kingdom of Korea one has to look for it towards the West, that is in the Bay of Nanking, at a latitude of about 40 degrees North. There a large river flows into the sea. This river passes about 1/2 mijl away from the city of Seoul. Here all the rice and all other revenues for the king arrive on big junks. The warehouses are about 8 mijl up the river. From there everything is transported on carts to the city.

The King holds court in the city of *Seoul*. Most of the nobles stay there as do the most prominent merchants, trading with China and Japan. Merchandise is first brought into Seoul and then retailed throughout the country. Here too, much trade is done with silver, since most of it is in the hands of the prominent people. In other towns and in the countryside trading is done with linen and cereals.

The reason for approaching Korea from the West coast is that along the South and the East coasts there are many cliffs and reefs, both visible and invisible, lying in and in front of the bays. Korean navigators told us that the West coast is best.

NOTES:

1. "As Benedictus de Klerk told me personally, Korea is densely populated." (Witsen, 47).
2. This must be *Hakata.*
3. "Mattheus Eibokken, one of those who in 1653 were taken prisoner in Korea, told me personally that generally speaking travel overland from Manchuria is quite impossible, because of the height of the mountains and the wildness of the nature. But a passage to Korea from Manchuria must exist, because during his stay the emperor of China sent the king of Korea 6 horses from Manchuria. He personally had witnessed their arrival." (Witsen, 44).
4. "As a confirmation about Dutch harpoons found in whales, I spoke with Benedictus Klerk, from Rotterdam, who had been a prisoner in Korea for 13 years. He confirmed that he had been present when these harpoons were extracted from a whale. He had recognized the harpoons, because as young men he and some other mates had left Holland to fish. Moreover he said that Koreans had special whalers and tackle for catching whales. Thus he and his comrades concluded there had to be a passage between Novaya Zemlya and Spitsbergen, at least for fish to swim through. Korean sailors said there was open sea to the Northeast. They thought that it might be easier to discover that passage from the Asian side. Small boats arrived daily from Northern Manchuria, bringing fish native to the North Sea, such as herring. Thus Mr. Klerk concluded that Asia and America are not attached at this side." (Witsen, 43-44).
5. Koreans know how to make very good salt from seawater. The Dutchmen cured herring there, which practice was unknown (Witsen, 57).
   Benedictus Klerk told me that "Herring is eaten unscaled and is being sold, laced in bundles of ten; the nets to that end are made of plaited straw" (ibid, 47)
6. The strait between Novaya Zemlya and the islands to the South in Russian is called *Wajgats.*
7. "Panax ginseng; is the medicine par excellence, the dernier ressort when all other drugs fail.... The principal Chinese name is derived from a fancied ressemblance to the human form. The genuine ginseng of Manchuria, whence the largest supplies are derived—in the remote mountains—consists of a stem from which the leaves spring, of a central root, and of two roots branching off. The roots are covered with rings, from which the age is ascertained, and the precious qualities are increased by age.... In 1891 Korean ginseng was worth Tls. 10.14 per catty...." (Couling, Encycl. Sinica, 1917, 206). "Wild Manchurian ginseng is almost worth its weight in gold. Even the semiwild quality from Corea is worth its weight in silver.... Though usually described

as a medicine, it is rather a food tonic, possessing, in the Chinese opinion, marvellous 'repairing' qualities." (Parker, *China, Past and Present*, 273).

8. "The court of the King is about as large as the city of Alkmaar, enclosed by a wall built up with stones and clay, on top incisions of stones, as if it were cockscombs. Within the court are a number of dwellings, very large ones and small ones, and all kinds of pleasure gardens. There also his spouse lives and the concubines, because he has, like everyone but one true wife. The King of Korea in this time was a coarse and strong man, it was said that he could bend a bow keeping the string under his chin and pull the bow with one hand." (Witsen, 59). It was during the reigns of King *Hyojong* (1649-1659) and King *Hyonjong* (1659-1674) that Hamel and his men spent 13 years of captivity in Korea. "Nominally sovereign of the country, he is held by powerful nobles intrenched in privileges hoary with age, and backed by all the reactionary influence of feudalism." (Griffis, *Corea*, 1905, 228-229).

9. Hamel speaks about the 'Tartar', meaning the Manchus.

10. Flintlocks are unknown. They do not use guns with a fuse. They use leather guns, covered on the inside with copper sheets, about 65 mm thick. The many layers of leather range from 5 to 12 cm thick. The guns are transported on one horse, following the army. These guns are about 1.7 m long and with these they are able to shoot fairly large cannon-balls. (Witsen, 56).

Mattheus Eibokken said, "Junks are equipped with countless small pieces of iron, and armed with a large number of firearms". (ibid, 50) This seems to be a reference to the famous turtleboat, the *kŏbuksŏn* (see Underwood *Korean Boats and Ships*, the Turtle Boat of Yi Sun Shin).

Along their beaches there are everywhere watch-towers standing in groups of four. If a fire is lighted on the first one, this means a small emergency, but in case the danger becomes greater, the fires on the second, third, and fourth towers are lighted. (ibid, 59)

11. There seem to be three distinct classes or grades of bonzes. The student monks devote themselves to learning, to study, and to the composition of books and the Buddhist ritual, the *tai-sa* being the abbot. The *jung* are mendicant and travelling bonzes, who solicit alms and contributions for the erection and maintenance of the temples and monastic establishments. The military bonzes (*siung kun*) act as garrisons, and make, keep in order, and are trained to use weapons (Griffis, *Corea*, 1905, 333).

12. The ceremony of *pul-tatta* or "receiving the fire" is undergone upon taking the vows of the priesthood. A moxa or cone of burning tinder is laid upon the man's arm, after the hair has been shaved off. The tiny mass is then lighted, and slowly burns into the flesh, leaving a painful sore, the scar of which remains as a mark of holiness. This serves as initiation, but if vows are broken, the torture is repeated on each occasion. In this manner, ecclesiastical

discipline is maintained (Griffis, *Corea*, 1905, 335).

13. Taoism, which divides Chinese attention with Buddhism, is almost unknown in Corea (Ross, *History Corea*, 355).

14. The twentieth King was *Hyonjong*, born in Moukden. He razed the Buddhist nunneries (Parker, "Corea", China Review XIV, 63).

15. Mattheus Eibokken informed me that people in Korea have a heathen faith, somewhat like the one in China, but nobody is coerced in matters of faith. They tolerated that the other Dutch prisoners mocked the idols (Witsen, 55). In Korea one finds idols about as big as complete houses in Holland and it is peculiar that one sees in almost all their temples three statutes standing side by side, of equal shape and attire, the middle one always being the biggest. Mr. Eibokken judged that some shadow of the Holy Trinity was concealed in this (Ibid, 56-57).

    According to Klerk "these people are not unconscious of the fact that there is a God, they revere the devil out of fear. Monks wander throughout the country begging, and make pilgrimages." (Ibid, 47)

15 a. The roofs of the houses of persons of high rank consists of both regular tiles and tiles and tiles baked from porcelain-clay of different colours, hence presenting a pleasant sight. The ordinary houses are straw thatched. One may see roof trusses 20 feet long. (Witsen, 49)

    They are not well-acquainted with glass; their windows are covered with oiled paper. Objects made of glass like rummers, or small bottles, imported into Japan by Netherlanders and then brought over from Japan, were highly valued. They could not believe that in our country window-panes were made of glass. (ibid, 56)

    It is customary there to have ducts under the floors of the rooms. These ducts are about one foot high, and carry heat to the whole room from stoves outside it. (ibid, 57)

16. "Hospitality is considered one of the most sacred duties. It would be a grave and shameful thing to refuse a portion of one's meal with any person, known or unknown, who presents himself at eating-time.... The poor man whose duty calls him to make a journey to a distant place does not need to make elaborate preparations.... At night, instead of going to a hotel with its attendant expense, he enters some house, whose exterior room is open to any comer. There he is sure to find food and lodging for the night." (Griffis, *Corea*, 1905, 288-289).

    It is very safe to travel through the country, as the people are modest, gentle, goodnatured, compassionate, and polite. (Witsen, 58)

17. Every year the King visits the grave of his ancestors to make offerings and to organize a feast there in honour and for the well-being of those in the other life. Mr. Eibokken accompanied the King to the graveside, which is several

hundred years old. It is a hollow mountain, which one enters through an iron door. This place is about 6 to 8 mijl outside the capital city. The dead are lying in iron, or tin coffins. They are embalmed in such a way that they are kept free from decay for several hundred years. When a King or a Queen is entombed a young slave and female slave are left there. Before closing of the iron door some provisions are left for them. Once these are finished they have to die, in order to serve their master or mistress in the other life (Witsen, 56).

(This custom certainly did not exist in the Yi period. Eibokken's imagination seems to have run away with him. The tomb of each King was located at a different place; vide Wilbur Bacon "Tombs of the Yi Dynasty Kings and Queens" RAS Transactions XXXIII, 1957, pp. 1-40.)

17 a. Klerk: "Koreans are very fainthearted. Therefore they often hang themselves out of fright or fear. This is, however, deemed honourable there." (Witsen, 47)

Eibokken: "Koreans are extremely afraid of the Tartars and the Japanese, because they are very fainthearted — to such an extent that when a battle or fight is going to take place some hundreds hang themselves, out of fear, on the day before." (ibid, 58)

Koreans of high rank are in the habit of having small pouches of poison attached to their girdles. If in their opinion necessity requires it, they can at once do away with themselves. (ibid, 59)

Ladies of distinction wear veils, and conceal themselves from unknown men. (ibid, 58)

The Koreans are very clean and tidy, when they make water they do so squatting. It is generally their habit to marry only once, but when a wife dies they take a concubine, the majority of the women there may be taken as such. (ibid, 59)

They eat with spoons as well as chopsticks. (ibid, 50)

Klerk refers to the preparation of *kimch'i*: "they have a custom there of pickling food of all kinds, especially tuberous plants." (ibid, 47)

18. "In 1651, a decree was issued ordering the people to use coin and at the same time prohibiting them from the use of cloth as money. Up to this time there had always been a party opposed to the use of coin that took every opportunity to suppress its use and replace it with rice and cloth. Now this party was fast disappearing and though they once more succeeded five years later in causing the rescission of the order to use coin, the people by that time had become so accustomed to its use that they began to coin for themselves. In 1678... rice and cloth were deprived forever of their monetary function." (M. Ichihara, "Coinage of Old Korea", Transactions of R.A.S., Korea Branch, 1913, Part II, 61).

They do not use coins, but pay in small ingots according to weight. (Witsen, 57)

19. All foreigners are refused admittance to this country with the exception of the Japanese, who have a settlement for their own use in the city of Pusan. (Witsen, 57)

Earthenware is made very well there, and especially bowls of rugged appearance, having been decorated as per order, are highly valued and in great demand in Japan, as the delicacy of Korean pottery surpasses that of Japan, it is mostly made by women. (ibid, 59)

The silks which are woven there are very beautiful. (ibid, 50)

One sees there fields entirely occupied by mulberry trees for the production of silk. (ibid, 50)

In this country much silk is produced, but no foreigners buy it, for which reason it is very cheap, but by way of Tsushima there is now some trade with the Japanese, which is annoying to the Netherlands' silk trade in Japan. (ibid, 59)

Very able artisans are to be found. The women, too, are skilful at embroidery; Eibokken had seen entire battles embroidered on silk, (ibid, 57)

"The Coreans had a third of their tribute remitted in 1643... and in the following year, when sending home the King's son, who had gone to Peking to have his title to the crown confirmed, a half was remitted... *Kanghi, Yoongjung,* and *Kienloong,* frequently remitted the tribute, demanding only a tithe, treating the Coreans like Chinese." (Ross, *History Corea,* 288). "A yearly or half-yearly tribute is sent in to Peking, accompanied by a host of merchants, who bring back profits much greater than the amount of the tribute." (Ibid, 365).

20. Mr. Eibokken had seen gold and silver mines, as well as copper, tin and iron mines. There is a large quantity of silver. Concessions to mine were given to special people. The King receives taxes from this. The copper in Korea is very bright and of a clear sound. He had seen gold veins in mines, and he had even dug up some golddust from some riverbeds. Goldmines are not opened as much as silver mines and those of other metal. The reason for this was not known to him (Witsen, 58).

Diamonds are not found there, but occasionally one comes across them and they are highly valued. (ibid, 50) Saltpetre is produced there in abundance. Quicksilver is also found there. (ibid, 58) In that country there are emeralds, sapphires and other precious stones which are unknown here. (ibid, 58)

The soil is everywhere cultivated. From wheat and rice good beverages are made, comparable in taste to Spanish wine. There are quite a number of islands off the mainland, and on some of them tobacco is cultivated, on others horses are raised for breeding. (ibid, 50) Grapes grow there, but rarely they ripen completely, and wine is not made from them. Pruning trees is not a custom there, and they do not know how to cultivate fruit. There is a certain fruit called canoen (*kam* = persimmon) which is very tasty when dried and resembles a fig. (ibid, 50) There are many kinds of fruit in Korea, most of them known in our country as well as many others, such as nuts, chestnuts, cherries, morelloes, quinces, pomegranates, rice, oats, wheat, beans, salad, and various tuberous plants. There are lots of poultry, pheasants and tortoises on land. (ibid, 57)

21. The climate is undoubtedly one of the finest and healthiest in the world. Foreigners are not afflicted by any climatic maladies (Isabella Bird, *Korea and Her Neighbours*, 1897, 16).

    There are rather good surgeons among them. (Witsen, 57) Important people let some of their slaves (some keep a few hundred of them) learn the healing art, but if the gentleman in question dies, the surgeon rarely survives him for long. (ibid, 59) They are very much afraid of sick people; they often bring them out into the fields and leave them alone in hovels, so that there is hardly anybody who tends and treats them. (ibid, 57)

22. There are fine horses and people ride these as in our country, not like the Tartars. On some islands they raise horses by letting them roam about freely. (Witsen I, 58).

    There is an abundance of cattle, but they hardly partake of butter and cheese, and even less of milk, saying that this is the blood of animals. Dogs — with the exception of red ones — as well as horses are eaten, as they judge these animals to have very tasty meat. (ibid, 57)

23. They write with brushes like the Chinese. It is said that once a Tartar envoy visiting the court asked by what means the kingdom was protected and ruled, and the King replied, "By the brush". Thereupon the Tartar took an arrow from hiw quiver and said, "Herewith we protect and rule our country". (Witsen, 58) [an interesting dialogue which cannot be checked, Dr. Vos]

    As far as Mr. Eibokken could judge, the Korean language has nothing in common with Chinese. Speaking Korean very well, he was not understood by the Chinese in Batavia, but they can read one another's writing. They have more than one way of writing, *Oonjek* (= ŏnyŏk, actual meaning 'translation <from the Chinese> into *hangul*. Dr. Vos) is a way of writing, like our running hand, all letters being linked. Common people use this. The other syllables are identical with the Chinese writing. (ibid, 59)

    The art of printing has been known to them — so they say — for more than 1,000 years. (Witsen, 56) it is a custom there to sing of all kinds of events in ballads, and every day therefore one hears songs about the deeds of heroes of ancient and recent times. Their printed books are full of these. (ibid, 56) [This must be a reference to the *kwangdae*, professional entertainers 'who recreated, dramatized, and sang known tales and narratives'. They were especially active in Chŏlla-do. See Peter J. Lee, Korean Literature: Topics and Themes, p. 86.]

"The poorer women though never at school, they can all, or almost all, use the Corean alphabet, which is the most beautiful and complete we know; for one can learn it almost at a sitting." (Ross, 315).

24. The King is so seldom seen that those who live far away believe he is super-human. They questioned us about him. The less the King rides out and is seen by the people, the more fruitful they consider the year to be. If he shows him-self not even a dog may walk the streets (Witsen, 57).

    The King may not be looked in the face by the common inhabitants. When he approaches everybody must conceal his face or turn around. (ibid, 58)

25. "The King rarely leaves the palace to go abroad in the city or country. When he does, it is a great occasion which is previously announced to the public. The roads are swept clean and guarded to prevent traffic or passage while the royal cortege is moving. All doors must be shut and the owner of each house is obliged to kneel before his threshold with a broom and dust-pan in his hands as emblems of obeisance. All windows, especially the upper ones, must be sealed with slips of paper, lest someone should look down on his majesty. Those who think they have received unjust punishment enjoy the right of appeal to the sovereign. They stand by the roadside tapping a small flat drum of hide streched on a hoop like a battledore. The king as he passes hears the prayer or receives the written petition held in a split bamboo." (Griffis, *Corea*, 1905, 222).

A pinas-ship like the "Sperwer".
The boatswain handles the capstan, while the navigation officer is giving instructions to the crew. Etching by Reinier Nooms (1652).

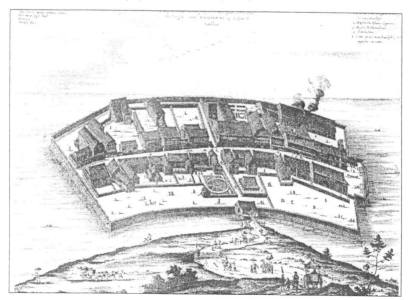

The Dutch trading-post at Deshima (Nagasaki)
Illustration from A. Montanus, VOC in Japan, Amsterdam 1669

VERHAAL

VAN HET VERGAAN VAN HET JACHT

DE SPERWER

EN VAN HET WEDERVAREN DER SCHIPBREUKELINGEN OP HET
EILAND QUELPAERT EN HET VASTELAND VAN KOREA (1653—1666)
MET EENE BESCHRIJVING VAN DAT RIJK

DOOR

HENDRIK HAMEL

UITGEGEVEN DOOR B. HOETINK

MET 1 KAART EN 11 AFBEELDINGEN

'S-GRAVENHAGE

MARTINUS NIJHOFF

1920

FURTHER DEVELOPMENTS

More than a year separated the final departure for Batavia from the day of the interview on their arrival in Nagasaki. The lives of Hamel and his men were not in danger anymore, they were well-fed and clothed, but for men used to wandering about the mountains of Chŏllado, who had had a boat of their own to row among the islands of Korea's South Sea, it must have felt as if they were in a prison after all. Confined as they were to the well-guarded, fan-shaped island, Deshima, about 170 m long and 100 m wide, their stay must have seemed very long.

Hamel used his time to write out his journal. While in captivity in Korea he certainly must have made notes about events, names and places. The names of the series of towns and fortresses they had passed through on their way up to Seoul would have been impossible to recall after 13 years. Some salvaged books had been given back to Hamel while he was still on Cheju island. The ship's logbook might have been among these. "11 August, rain coming from the S.E.. We are heading N.E. by E.N.E." reads like an entry copied straight from the logbook.

It is interesting to follow the events of arrival and departure from the notices in the Daily Register, written by the head of the Dutch trading post at Deshima, Mr. Wilhelm Volger:

> 14 September 1666: Tuesday...for the past three days there have been rumors circulating about 8 Europeans, oddly dressed, having landed in the Goto islands in a strange craft. Now they are on their way to Nagasaki. Every hour the same story comes up with so many changing circumstances, that one does not know what to think about it, even less how to write about it. Early this morning we were told that the vessel with the men had arrived last night. After having been interrogated by the governor, they were sent to us on the island at one o'clock in the afternoon. They are

eight Dutchmen: Hendrik Hamel from Gorkum, Govert Denijs from Rotterdam and his son Denijs Goverts, Matthijs Eibocken from Enkhuizen, Jan Pieters from Heerenveen, and Gerrit Jans and Benedictus Clerck from Rotterdam.

I will not recount all they experienced in Korea. Twenty of their men died over there, and eight men still remain in different places in Korea. The governor of Nagasaki suggested through the interpreters that we had better celebrate their rescue and said that he would write to Edo (Tokyo) about it. It is remarkable that after eight months stranded on Quelpaert Island, an elderly man, looking like a Dutchman (apparently sent there by the King of Korea), after a long while finally asked them in broken Dutch who they were, and then he said that he too was from Holland, born in De Rijp and that his name was Jan Jansz Weltevree and that he had been living in Korea for 26 years. He is still alive and more than 70 years old.

17 October 1666: Requested the governor to let the eight Dutchmen who arrived here last month to depart for Batavia, which was not allowed, saying that no answer from Edo had arrived yet, but that an answer could be expected every hour. Meanwhile the ships will sail tomorrow and these poor people might have to stay here for another year, which would be deplorable. [Vessels departed for Batavia only once each year.]

On 18 October 1666, an official letter was dispatched by Wilhelm Volger, Daniel Six, Nicolaes de Roij, and Daniel van Vliet to His Excellency Joan Maetsuycker, Governor General, and to the Council of the Indies, in which it was reported: "Through the irresistible and unbounded hand of God, last month eight persons from the Korean islands miraculously arrived here, having been shipwrecked on Quelpaert Island with the Sperwer in 1653. Among them is the book-keeper Hendrik Hamel and seven sailors. Eight other persons still remain in Korea. Those who arrived here will sail to Batavia on the *Esperance*."

Mr. Volger left Deshima on the *Esperance* a few days later. He wrote in his report:

It turned out that those poor men had to stay behind. When I took leave from the governor of Nagasaki and asked permission for them to leave as well, this was flatly denied, the governor saying there had been no order from the court at Edo, and that they might even have to come up to Edo before receiving permission to leave Deshima. Meanwhile for these afflicted souls it will be difficult to stay another year before they are able to enjoy their freedom.

The new man in charge, Mr. Daniel Six, wrote as follows on 25 October 1666:

This morning around 9 o'clock the interpreters summoned the eight Dutchmen to come to the governor's office. I called for the men and ordered them to go with the interpreters. What questions these presumptuous Japanese regents will ask we shall learn upon their return. Shortly after noon they returned to the island and the book-keeper Hendrik Hamel reported that in the presence of the Governor they were asked: first, their names and ages, then the life and manners of the Koreans, the kind of clothes they wore, their army, way of life and religion, if there were Portugese and Chinese living there, as well as how many Dutchmen remained, and so on. After having answered each of these questions to their contentment, they were ordered to return to the island.

In an appendix to his journal, Hamel wrote: "25 October 1666: Having been called again before the old and the new Governor, the aforementioned questions were asked to each of us in particular and answered as before."

One year later, Hamel wrote:

"22 October 1667: around noon, the new Governor having arrived, we were granted license to depart. Towards evening we embarked on the *Spreeuw* in order to leave for Batavia in convoy with the *Witte Leeuw*."

"23 October 1667: at the dawn of day the anchor was weighed and we sailed out of the bay of Nagasaki"

In the Deshima register for Saturday, 22 October 1667, is found the following:

Notwithstanding heavy rains, today the *Witte Leeuw* and the *Spreeuw* have set sail for Batavia. This morning we received a licence that the eight persons from Korea could leave. In spite of the fact that the new Governor of Nagasaki had arrived several days ago, we had not yet received the permit allowing the eight Dutchmen who arrived here last year to leave. They will embark on the *Spreeuw*.

A little more than a month later the party finally arrived in Batavia. Hamel concluded his journal:

> "On [28 November 1667] we arrived at the Roads of Batavia. The good Lord be given thanks that by His Grace we were freed from the hands of the heathens, having roamed about in great misery and sadness during 14 years and now having returned to our people."

In the manuscript, the date had not been entered, but the following entry appears in the daily register of Batavia:

> "28 November 1667: arrived here from Japan the vessels *Spreeuw* and *Witte Leeuw*".

Hamel and the seven sailors met with the Council of the Indies on 2 December and requested restitution of their salaries. The head of the trading post at Deshima had written an appeal asking that the Council take pity on the escapees. However the plea was in vain. If a ship was lost, its crew ceased to be paid. This was the rule. Their payment was restored only from the day they arrived in Nagasaki. For some who were still boys when first engaged, wages were raised by a few guilders to 9 guilders a month. Hamel remained in Batavia, while the other seven sailors continued their voyage homeward.

Once back in Holland, they again tried to claim back pay from the directors in Amsterdam, but with no more success. Out of compassion, as a compensation for the years spent in Korea, a gratuity of fl. 1,530 was authorized and was divided among them.

The Colonial Archives (No. 255) contain the following entries:

> 11 August 1668: Have met the men who spent 13 years and 28 days in captivity in Korea. They handed over a written report, which we will read and examine, then a decision will be made.

> 13 August 1668: Listened to the reading of the report of the committee who read the Journal about what had happened during the Korean captivity, as well as the description of that country. We decided to write to the Council of the Indies, that we would be willing to send a delegate over

there, and enter into trade relations, if the Council would have no objections. Moreover, we decided that the seven men, out of compassion, will receive 1,530 guilders, apportioned as follows:

Govert Denijs, (fl. 14 per month)	fl. 300
Mattheus Ybocken, (fl. 14 per month)	fl. 300
Jan Pietersz, (fl. 11 per month)	fl. 250
Gerrit Jansz, (fl. 9 per month)	fl. 200
Cornelis Dircksz, (fl. 8 per month)	fl. 180
Dionijs Govertsz, (fl. 5 per month)	fl. 150
Benedictus Clercq, (fl. 5 per month)	fl. 150

Four of the above-mentioned men were from Rotterdam. A brief glance at the fortunes of those whose names recur in *Hamel's Journal* discloses that the oldest man of the group was Govert Dionyssen (Denijszen), 47 years old at the interview, born in 1619. As a young widower he had married a second time on 1 December 1647. The bride was Annetje Alewijns van Pinckeveer, also from Rotterdam. Their wedding was registered at the city hall and not in a church. From the Record Office we learn that on 11 March 1645 he had declared himself to be a citizen of Rotterdam, about 26 years old and then he made a statement about the death of a sailor on a return voyage from the Indies. He made this declaration: "met waere woorden in plaetse van solempnelen eede" (with affirmation of truth instead of a solemn oath), indicating that he was either a Mennonite or a Quaker. Rotterdam has always had an important Mennonite community. The youngest member of the party, Denijs Govertszen, was his son, from the first marriage. Both father and son had arrived in the Indies in 1651 on the *Nieuw Rotterdam*. At the time, Denijs was a mere child, only 10 years old.

From the Record Office of the city of Rotterdam we learn that the ship's boy Benedictus Clercq left Batavia on 23 December 1667 on the ship *Vreyheyt* (Liberty) and arrived in Holland on 19 July 1668. A notarial deed (No. 389, 341-342) states: "Benedictus Clercq, recently returned from the East Indies on the ship *Vreyheyt*, was present on 23 July 1668 at the notary office of Mr. Jacob Delphius, authorizing master Jan Tyssen to receive on his behalf the amount of 37 guilders and 10 five-cent pieces." He then signed the deed with an 'X', for he could not write. This was the humble mark of a young man who had served as bodyguard to the King of Korea, who had endured all of the ups and downs of the long years in captivity, and who had spent nearly half of his life in Korea—he was 27 years old at the time of the interview in Nagasaki. He had arrived in the Indies in 1651 on the *Zeelandia*, as a boy 12 years old, earning 5 guilders a month. Once back in his hometown of Rotterdam he married Marja Sijbers and in the following years baptisms of five of his children were recorded in the registers of the Reformed Church. His wife died in 1709, however the death of Mr. Clercq is not recorded in Rotterdam.

The fourth man from Rotterdam, Gerrit Janszen, had arrived in the Indies in 1648, as a ship's boy on the *Zeelandia*. His salary had been raised to 10 guilders a month.

It must have been a very difficult decision for the men stranded in Korean to decide who among them should join in the escape and who should remain. In the *journal* we read that Jan Pieterszen was asked to join as he was an experienced navigator. Hamel was the only remaining officer, Mattheus Eibocken and Cornelis Dirckse were asked to join and then there were the above-mentioned four men from Rotterdam, among whom were the father and son. From the interview we learn that the party decided to escape without informing the others about the plan. Their departure was kept secret because the boat was not large enough for all. Moreover, twice each month men had to present themselves at the commander's office, and with some men left behind, their escape would not have been noticed straightaway.

Concerning the men who remained behind in *Chŏlla* province, Hamel offers no further word. He could not. So it was that as late as 1905 Griffis still could write in his book on Korea: "The fate of the other survivors of the Sparrow Hawk crew was never known. Perhaps it never will be learned." (176) In the Transactions of the R.A.S. Korea Branch, Vol. 9, 1918, Mark Napier Trollope, the Anglican Bishop in Korea and President of the Royal Asiatic Society, introduced the account of Hendrik Hamel and wrote: "One of the unfortunate mariners who did not succeed in making his escape was Alexander Bosquet, a Scotchman. One wonders if his tomb or those of any of his mates will ever come to light". (94-95) Nowadays we know better and know that Mr. Bosquet was not from Scotland at all. Sander Boesquet was a Hollander, from a small town called Lith. All through the old documents one sees that there is no uniform spelling of proper names, family or given.

In an official document of the VOC (United East India Company) dated 16 September 1668, it is mentioned that after the escape of Hamel and his companions two years earlier, Jan Claeszen from Dordrecht, the oldest of all the captives, had died. However, Nicolaas Witsen wrote: "The remaining men, through the intercession of the Emperor of Japan at the behest of the VOC, have been handed over, except one, who wanted to remain there. He preferred to stay in that country of strangers. He had been married over there and pretended that he no longer had a hair on his body to identify him as a Christian, or a Dutchman." (Witsen, 53) Whether the Korean authorities would have accepted this is doubtful.

A detailed account of how the remaining men made their way to Japan is given in Ledyard's *The Dutch Come to Korea* (83-97). Once again Jan Janse Weltevree was involved, he must have been about 72 years old by that time. When the Korean authorities investigated the escape of Hamel and his companions, they questioned Weltevree in Seoul in January 1667 about his own arrival in Korea more than 26 years before and how he then had been sent away from the Japanese lodge at Pusan. They used this information in their negotiations with the Japanese officials.

The seven remaining Dutchmen were ordered to assemble in Namwon. Each of them received a coat, ten catties of rice, two pieces of linen and other presents and then they departed Korea via the Japanese trading post at Tongnae (Pusan) in July 1668. "The Japanese government had always made use of Tsushima in its communications with the Coreans, and the agency in Fusan was composed exclusively of retainers of the feudal lord of this island." (Griffis, 86) Due to bad weather they arrived in Nagasaki only on 16 September 1668.

Their names were: Jacob Lampen, assistant, from Amsterdam; Hendrik Cornelissen, in charge of ropes etc. from Vlieland; Jacob Jansen, quartermaster, from Flekeren; Zander Baskit, gunner, from Lith; Anthony Uldriksen, sailor, from Grieten; Jan Jansen Spelt, gunner, from Utrecht; and Cornelis Arentsen, boy, from Oosta'pen.

These men too were interrogated by the Japanese authorities about Korea and the commercial relations between Japan and Korea. Then the seven men received permission to leave Japan. Their ship, the *Nieuwpoort*, left Nagasaki on 27 October 1668. They arrived on 8 April 1669 in Batavia, their vogage having been via Coromandel. In Batavia they were reunited with Hendrik Hamel and in 1670 they all returned to Holland.

On 29 August 1670 three of them met with the directors at the head office of the VOC in Amsterdam: "Hendrik Hamel, from Gorinchem, Hendrik Cornelis Molenaar, from Vlieland, and Jan Jansz Spelt, from Utrecht, having been detained 15 years in Korea, requested payment for the time of their detention, or as judged reasonable. Following the precedent of the resolution of 13 August 1668, these persons, as well as some others in the same situation, will be paid accordingly" (VOC Resolutions, Colonial Archives, No. 256).

Concerning trade relations with Korea, on 18 December 1610, Prince Maurits of Nassau, Stadholder of Holland, who later became the Prince of Orange, had already written a letter to the Japanese emperor asking for permission to be allowed to sail the Japanese north coast and to trade with Korea. This letter was written in vain, although Richard Cocks wrote in his diary on 30 November 1630: "The Flemynges...have som small entrance allready into Corea, per way of an iland called Tushma, which standeth within sight of Corea and is frend to the Emperor of Japan." (*Diary of Richard Cocks* II, 258)

The English, who were rivals of the Dutch, had no better luck. Captain John Saris wrote on 17 October 1614: "I make noe doubt but your seruant Edward Sares is by this tyme in Corea, for from Tushina I appoynted him to goe thither, beinge incouradged by the Chineses that our broad cloath was in greater request ther than hear. It is but 50 leagues ouer from Iapann and from Tushina much less." (*The Voyage of Captain John Saris to Japan*, 210) However, Richard Cocks wrote on 25 November 1614: "We cannot per any meanes get trade as yet from

Tushma into Corea, nether have them of Tushma any other privelege but to enter into one little towne (or fortresse), and in paine of death not to goe without the walles thereof to the landward." (270) According to a letter written in Firando (*Hirado*) on 9 March 1614, "Sayer is out of hope of any good to be done there [in Tsushima] or at Corea." (*Letters Written by the English Residents in Japan*, 130)

After the return of Hamel, a new attempt was made to open up trade relations, but Batavia advised against such a plan, which the authorities of China and Japan certainly would have opposed. It was decided that as long as "we have in Japan our residence and trade, we should forget about the idea of doing any trade in Korea, in order not to rouse any jealousy or mistrust in the Japanese, not to mention the fact that the Chinese would not tolerate us being there. We should put it out of our thoughts, but with success and the changing of time, one does not know what might come from it in the future." A farsighted decision!

Above the name Benedicties Clercq is marked an "X". (Archives, Rotterdam)

ABOUT THE AUTHOR AND
THE DIFFERENT EDITIONS OF THE TEXT

Critics who remark that *Hamel's Journal* is not learned or even entirely reliable in its descriptions certainly are correct. But what could one expect from a young man who left Holland at the age of 20 and worked in the Indies for two years before embarking on the unfortunate last voyage of the *Sperwer*? All the ensuing years in Korea were lived in hardship, without books, in isolation from the outside world, surrounded by an unknown culture. One wonders, however, if we would have learned more from him if Hamel had been an academic instead of a ship's bookkeeper. Griffis introduces him as follows in his 1905 study, *Corea*: "Hamel, the supercargo of the ship, wrote a book on his return, recounting his adventures in a simple and straightforward style." Maybe he would not have written this unadorned account of what took place and given so uncomplicated a description of the land and people of Korea had he been a man of learning.

Seventeenth century geographical works often were culled from various sources, which were copied and then decorated with personal opinions. The writer, who is here often mentioned in the footnotes, is Nicolaes Witsen (1641-1717) and his book "Noord-en Oost Tartarye" (North- and East Tartary), first edition 1692, second edition 1705. All quotations are from the second edition. Since the Middle Ages 'Tartary' had been the designation of Central Asia. Witsen's book was meant as a textual guide to a great map he had published, which included present-day Siberia, Mongolia, Korea and China. Witsen had numerous official duties: he was thirteen times Burgomaster of Amsterdam, Treasurer, Counsellor and Deputy of the States General, board member of the VOC (the Dutch East India Company), Commissioner of Pilotage, etc. In his

Nicolaes Witsen *by Francis van Bossuet (1653-1717)*
Collection Victoria and Albert Museum, London

library there were many works on foreign countries and peoples, as well as manuscripts by authors who were employed by the VOC. It is often unclear from where he got his information.

"Noord-en Oost Tartarye" consists almost exclusively of separate notes strung together, using many sources: publications, diaries, oral statements, reports, etc.

For his description of Korea Witsen made use of several publications about China and Japan, as well as a report of the Dutch court-journey to Edo in 1637 with a description of the Korean embassy to Japan, and of the eye-witness accounts of the undersurgeon Mattheus Eibokken and Benedictus Klerk, whose names are given (in the second edition).

The question then is: when did he meet with the two Hamel companions? The sailors had returned to Amsterdam in August 1668 when they met with the board of the VOC. At that time Nicolaes Witsen was still a young man of twenty-seven, who had recently been to Moscow (1664-1665). How could we picture their meeting? The scholarly, rich young man, with a brilliant future and the ship's boy Klerk, who was about the same age, who had spend half of his life in Korea, who could not even sign his name, but who could tell him that 'Asia and America are not attached at this side'.

Witsen married in 1674 and his first appointment as Burgomaster of Amsterdam was in 1682. The publication of the first edition of his book on Tartary, in which 'the Dutchmen having been captives in Korea' are mentioned, was in 1692, but nowhere did he mention Hamel's name. The second edition, in which Eibokken and Klerk are often mentioned, was published only in 1705. Thirtyseven years after their return to the Netherlands!

Witsen's information is often very unsystematic, but adds unexpected glimpses into daily life in Korea in the middle of the seventeenth century. In the footnotes a number are brought together per subject.

Comparing Hamel's narrative with Witsen's compiled study, we can say that Hamel's writing was at least original.

What pleases many readers of Hamel's journal is his candid acknowledgement of the good treatment he and his mates had received in most of their encounters with an unknown and "heathen" people. The simplicity with which he recounts his experience and makes his observations show his sincerity. Nowhere can one observe a deliberate misdescription. If there are mistakes they are honest ones.

Looking at what Hamel wrote about Korean houses and gardens, one finds in the Churchill edition: "There being generally before the Houses of the nobility a large square, or Bass Court, with a Fountain, or Fish-Pond, and a garden with covered walks." In his manuscript Hamel wrote: "De edelluyden hebben voor haar huysen gemeenelijck een groote plaats, waar vijver ende thuyn is, versiert met veele bloemen ende andere rarigheden, van bomen en clippen..." which translates as: "(The nobility) generally have in front of their houses a large inner court with a pond and a garden, decorated with many flowers and other rare plants, trees and rocks." The difference may be of no immense importance, but persons who have lived in Korea know the importance of rocks in a Korean garden, while the European translator did not know what to make of the reference, and so the rocks somehow became covered walkways. This is but one example of how precisely Hamel wrote down what he saw.

Of course we would like to know much more about Hamel's life and that of his companions. He mentions no details about most of the deaths of the other men during their time in Chŏlla province. Nor does he say anything about living with Korean women or having children, perhaps out of discretion, for a number of the men had wives back in Holland. At least, personal attachments might explain why some of the seamen who returned to Amsterdam were so ready to go back to Korea, if ever commercial relations were established.

Viewing what we know about the crew of the *Sperwer* we read that after the shipwreck on Cheju island 36 men were alive. On the road to Seoul one man, Paulus Janse Cool, from Purmerend died in Yongam. During their stay in Seoul the chief navigation officer, Hendrick Janse, from Amsterdam and Hendrick Janse Bos, from Haarlem died in 1655. In 1656 arriving in Pyŏngyŏng, they number thirty-three. Seven years later, leaving Pyŏngyŏng, there were twenty-two men in all. Eleven must have died in Pyŏngyŏng. Three years later, after the escape, eight men remained in the Chŏlla province. Six more must have died: four men in Yosu and two in Namwon.

The sixteen survivors were: the writing of their names varies by source, as the writing of their town of origin.

Hendrik Hamel, from Gorinchem (born in)	1630
Govert Denijs, from Rotterdam	1619
Dionijs Govertsz (his son)	1641
Mattheus Ybocken, from Enkhuizen	1634
Jan Pietersz (de Vries), from Heerenveen	1630
Gerrit Jans, from Rotterdam	1634
Cornelis Dirksz, from Amsterdam	1635
Benedictus Clerck, from Rotterdam	1639
Johannes (Jacob) Lampen, from Amsterdam	1630
Hendrick Cornelis Molenaar, from Vlieland	1629
Jan Claes, from Dordrecht	1617
Jacob Jansen, from Vleekeren/Flekeren	1619
Sander Boesquet (Zandert Baskit), from Lith	1625
Jan Jansz. Spelt, from Utrecht	1631
Anthonie Uldircksz (Uldricksen), from Grieten	1634
Claes (Cornelis) Arentsen, from Oostvoort/Oosta'pen	1639
(maybe the German town of Apen?)	

At the time of his interview in Nagasaki in 1666, Hamel was 36 years old, he was born in 1630 (baptism 20 August). His family belonged to the bourgeoisie of the town of Gorinchem in Holland. He left the Netherlands on 6 November 1650 on the *Vogelstruys*, one of the largest ships then in use by the VOC, measuring about 1000 metric tons and carrying more than 300 passengers and crew. On 4 July 1651 he arrived at the Roads of Batavia. While working in Batavia (present day Jakarta, the capital of Indonesia), his salary was raised from the 10 guilders paid to him as a sailor to 30 guilders per month when he was promoted to assistant and then to book-keeper.

In 1670 he returned to Amsterdam after an absence of 20 years. He made a second voyage to the Indies and on 12 February 1692 he died in his hometown of Gorinchem, unmarried.

The first editions of his Journal were published quickly in 1668, in Amsterdam by *Van Velsen* and in Rotterdam by *Stichter*. One wonders if

Hamel even was informed about the publications, as the journal had been written as an internal company report. In the following year, 1669, in Amsterdam there appeared the *Saagman* edition, which was "embellished" with exotic elements such as crocodiles and elephants. It is this *Saagman* edition that was used for a French translation published in Paris in 1670. In 1672, a German edition was published in Nurnberg. An English text, translated from the translation into French, was published in London in 1704 in *A Collection of Voyages and Travels* in 4 volumes, edited by John Churchill (reprinted in Transactions of the R.A.S., Korea Branch, Vol. 9, 1918, and also in Gari Ledyard's study, *The Dutch Come to Korea*, Seoul, 1971). Besides the exotic elements, a number of errors and omissions compromised the text along the way. For instance, the phrase "[Korea] is van nature een seer gesont land" (is by nature a very healthy country) is one of numerous lines one cannot find in the Churchill edition, to say nothing of its many inaccuracies.

A Korean translation, also based on the French edition, was published in the 1930s and reprinted in Seoul in 1954 by *Ilchogak*, as *Hamel p'yo-ryugi* by Yi Pongdo, who supplemented the text with Korean and Japanese sources. In 1961-5, Ikuta Shigeru published a Japanese translation based on the Hamel manuscript, annotated and enlarged with Korean sources.

The present translation is based on the text in the *Hoetink* edition, which was published at The Hague in 1920 by the *Linschoten Society*. I have attempted this first translation into contemporary English from the 17th century Dutch manuscripts of *Hamel's Journal* and his *Description of the Kingdom of Korea* because I believe we owe it to Hendrik Hamel and Korea to make this first Western document on Korea more accessible. The author paid for it with more than 13 years of his young life.

The manuscript itself contains no subdivisions or editorial apparatus. The Churchill edition provides indications in the margin. I have highlighted the years. In the *Description of the Kingdom of Korea*, I have inserted section headings to facilitate reading; they do not belong to the original text. The *Hoetink* edition concludes with a short text, written after Hamel's return. This conclusion seems a fitting end to the description as it invites further discovery.

The isolation in which Korea persevered after Hamel's escape kept the respect for the existing order unimpaired and few changes were introduced in the life of the nation. When Korea was forced to open her gates to foreigners in the 19th century, it became possible to compare the country the newcomers observed with Hamel's observations of it two centuries earlier. His narrative had not become obsolete. In his "Stray Notes on Corean History, etc.," J. Scott wrote: "The narrative of the Dutch supercargo Hamel, gives a graphic account of Corean manners and customs and, as read at the present time, conveys an exact picture of people and country. Place after place which he mentions in their captive wanderings have been identified, and every scene and every feature can be recognised as if it were a tale told today. So strong is native conservatism both in language and habits that Hamel's description of two hundred years ago reproduces every feature of present Corean life" (*Journal of the China Branch of the Royal Asiatic Society*, 1893-94, 215).

The *Hoetink* edition quotes many of the early writings on Korea and many of these have been reproduced or cited in the notes to this translation.

All Korean geographical names are written in the modern romanized spellings and not in the phonetic forms Hamel himself employed.

From the manuscript: in the middle of the first line one sees Jan Jansz. Weltevree' from De Rijp, 1628, on the 7th line a correction 19 a 20 into 17 a 18 years.

HAMEL'S LIST OF KOREAN WORDS AND TRANSLITERATIONS

Korean words and names used by Hamel in a phonetic spelling (to the 17th century Dutch ear), the current romanization and meaning.

Tiocen Cock	Chosŏn-kuk	Korea
Jirpon	Ilbon	Japan
Jeenara	Oenara	derogatory name for Japan
Moggan	Mok-kwan	house of the mok-sa
Mocxo	Mok-sa	prefect
Tieckese	Taekuksa	Chinese
Oranckay	Orangkai	barbarian
Nampancoeck	Namban-kuk	Portugal
Nampancoy	Namban-kot	tobacco
Jipamsansiang	Ibamsansŏng	Ibam mountain fortress
Namhansansiang	Namhansansŏng	Namhan mountain fortress
Thiellado	Chŏlla-do	Cholla province
Tiongsiando	Chungch'ŏng-do	Chungchong province
Senggado	Kyŏnggi-do	Kyonggi province
Thella peing	Chŏlla Pyŏngyŏng	Cholla garrison
Peingsa	Pyŏng-sa	commandant
Sior	Seoul	place name
Pousaen	Pusan	" "
Scheluo	Cheju-do	" "
Tadjang	Taejŏng	" "
Heynam	Haenam	" "
Naedjoo	Naju	" "
Sansiangh	Changsŏng	" "

Tiongop	Chŏng-ŭp	"	"
Teyn	T'aein	"	"
Kninge	Kŭmku	"	"
Chentio	Chŏnju	"	"
Jehaen	Yŏsan	"	"
Gunjiu	Unjin	"	"
Jensoen	Yŏnsan	"	"
Chongtio	Kongju	"	"
Jeham	Yŏngam	"	"
Duytsiang	Taechang	"	big granary
Saysingh	Chwasuyŏng	"	left prov. naval district
Naysing	Naeyepo	"	
Sunischien	Sunch'ŏn	"	
Namman	Namwon	"	
Tymatte	Taima-do	" ·	Japanese island

Statue of Hendrick Hamel
by Jaap Hartman, 1997

MASTER EIBOKKEN ON THE KOREAN LANGUAGE

Oldest Western list of Korean words

Transactions, Royal Asiatics Society, Korea Branch, Volume L, 1975: p. 30-39.

Dr. Frits Vos

Professor of the Japanese and Korean Languages, Literature and History at the
University of Leyden in the Netherlands.

The most important contribution to Hamel's narrative is Eibokken's vocabulary of 143 Korean words as listed below. Words requiring additional commentary have been marked with an asterix and are given on the following pages.

Eibokken uses the following Dutch transcription for Korean vowels and diphthongs: *a* or *ae* for 아, *a* or *e* for ᄋ, *ey* for 애, or 익, *e* for ᄋ, 어, 에, and ᄋ, *o* for 어 or 오, *oo* for 오, *oe* (occasionally *ou*) for 우, *i, ie* or *y* for 이. Dutch *j* (and sometimes *i*) corresponds to English *y*, e.g. *Jang* = *yang* 羊양 (nr. 75), *piaer — pyŏl* (64).

For *k* as a medial or final he nearly always writes *ck*. Instead of *n* he sometimes writes *d* (cf. nrs. 4, 14, 108). Because of typographical errors an original *u* may have been rendered as *n* (cf. nrs. 16, 19).

Several items in Eibokken's vocabulary evoke rather interesting speculations and observations.

*　*　*　*

[The way of] counting in *Korea*, among persons of high rank, is — from one to ten — as follows:[98]

---

[98]If the pronunciation of the word in question in the 17th century was different, it is listed first under the heading 'Corrections in transcription' and followed by the transcription of the modern pronunciation. These readings are separated by a slash mark (/). My *ă* stands for ᄋ, *ăe* for 익, In the case of dialect words the items in question are followed in the same way by the readings in modern standard Korean. At the end of the vocabulary furter explanations are listed according to the numbers preceding the words.

(original text)	(English or numerals)	(corrections in) transcription)	(corrections in translation)
1. *Ana*, een	one	*hăna/hana*	
2. *Taue* of *Toel*, twee	two	*tul (tu)*	
3. *Sevve* of *suy*, drie	three	*set (se)*	
4. *Deuye*, vier	four	*net (ne)*	
5. *Tasset*, vyf	five	*tasăt/tasŏt*	
6. *Joset* of *jacet*, zes	six	*yŏsăt/yŏsŏt*	
7. *Girgop* of *jirgop*, zeven	seven	*nilgop/ilgop*	
8. *Joderp* of *jadarp**, acht	eight	*yŏdălp, yŏdŭlp/yŏdŏl [p]*	
9. *Agop* of *ahob*, negen	nine	*ahop*	
10. *Iaer**, thien	ten	*yŏl*	
The common man counts as follows:			
11. *Jagnir**, een	one	*hăn il/han il*	
12. *Tourgy*, twee	two	*tul i*	
13. *Socsom*, drie	three	*sŏk sam*	
14. *Docso*, vier	four	*nŏk să/nŏk sa*	
15. *Caseto, vyf*	five	*tasăt o/tasŏt o*	
16. *Joseljone*, zes	six	*yŏsăt yuk/yŏsŏt yuk*	
17. *Jeroptchil*, zeven	seven	*nilgop ch'il/ilgop ch'il*	
18. *Jaderpal*, acht	eight	*yadal p'al/yŏdŏl [p] p'al*	
19. *Ahopcon*, negen	nine	*ahop ku*	
20. *Jorchip*, thien	ten	*yŏl sip*	
21. *Somer*, twintig	twenty	*sŭmŭl/sŭmul*	
22. *Schierri* of *siergan*, dertig	thirty	*sŏr[h]ŭn*	
23. *Mahan**, veertig	forty	*maăn/mahŭn*	
24. *Swin*, vyftig	fifty	*swin*	
25. *Jegu* of *jeswyn*, zestig	sixty	*yesyun/yesun*	
26. *Hierigum* of *jirgun*, zeventig	seventy	*nirhŭn/ir[h]ŭn*	
27. *Jadern* of *jadarn*, tachtentig	eighty	*yŏdŭn*	

(original text)	(English or numerals)	(corrections in transcription)	(corrections in translation)
28. *Haham* of *ahan*, negentig	ninety	*ahŭn*	
29. *Hirpee* of *jyrpeik**, honderd	100	*ilbăek/ilbaek*	
30. *Jijrpeyck*, twee honderd	200	*ibaek*	
31. *Sampeyck*, drie honderd	300	*sambaek*	
32. *Soopeyck*, vier honderd	400	*săbăek/sabaek*	
33. *Opeyck*, vyf honderd	500	*obaek*	
34. *Joeckpeyck*, zes honderd	600	*yukpaek*	
35. *t'Syrpeyck*, zeven honderd	700	*ch'ilbaek*	
36. *Paelpeyck*, acht honderd	800	*p'albaek*	
37. *Koepeyck*, negen honderd	900	*kubaek*	
38. *Jyrtcien**, een duizend	1000	*ilch'yŏn/ilch'ŏn*	
39. *Jijetcien*, twee duizend	2000	*ich'ŏn*	
40. *Samtcien*, drie duizend	3000	*samch'ŏn*	
41. *Sootcien*, vier duizend	4000	*săch'yŏn/sach'ŏn*	
42. *Otcien*, vyf duizend	5000	*och'ŏn*	
43. *Joecktcien*, zes duizend	6000	*yukch'ŏn*	
44. *t'Syertcien*, zeven duizend	7000	*ch'ilch'ŏn*	
45. *Paertcien*, acht duizend	8000	*p'alch'ŏn*	

(original text)	(English or numerals)	(corrections in transcription)	(corrections in translation)
46. *Koetcien*, negen duizend	9000	*kuch'ŏn*	
47. *Jyroock**, thien duizend	10,000	*ir'ŏk*	100,000
48. *Jyoock*, twintig duizend	20,000	*iŏk*	etc.
49. *Samoock*, dertig duizend	30,000	*sam'ŏk*	
50. *Soeoock*, veertig duizend	40,000	*săok/saŏk*	
51. *Ooock*, vyftig duizend	50,000	*oŏk*	
52. *Koeoock**, zestig duizend	60,000	*kuŏk*	900,000 (yug'ŏk)
53. *t'Siroock*, zeventig duizend	70,000	*ch'ir'ŏk*	
54. *Joeoock*, tachten- duizend	80,000	*yug'ŏk*	600,000
55. *Paeroock*, negentig duizend	90,000	*p'ar'ŏk*	800,000
56. *Jyoock**, honderd duizend	100,000	*chyo/cho*	one million

Some Korean terms follow.

57. *Pontchaa** is their name for God	God	*ponjon?*	
58. *Mool**, een Paerd	a horse	*mol, măl/mal*	
59. *Moolhoot**, meer Paerden	more horses	*mol. . . . ?*	
60. *Hiechep*, een Wyf	woman, wife (derogatory)	*kyejip*	
61. *Hanel**, Hemel	heaven	*hanăl/hanŭl*	
62. *Hay*, de Zon	the sun	*hăe/hae*	
63. *Tael*, de Maen	the moon	*tăl/tal*	
64. *Piaer*, de Sterren	the stars	*pyŏl*	
65. *Parram*, de Wind	the wind	*părăm/param*	

(original text)	(English or numerals)	(corrections in transcription)	(corrections in translation)
66. *Nam*, Zuiden	South		
67. *Poeck*, Noorden	North	*pŭk/puk*	
68. *Siuee*, West	West	*syŏ/sŏ*	
69. *Tong*, Oost	East		
70. *Moel*,'t Water	the water	*mŭl, mul*	
71. *Moet*, d'Aerde	the, earth	*mŭl, mut*	land, *terra firma*
72. *Moel koikie**, al-derhande soort van Vis	fish of all kinds	*mulkoegi, mŭlkogi/ mulkogi*	
73. *Moet koikie**, al-derhande soort van Vlees	meat of all kinds	*mutkoegi, mŭtkogi/ mutkogi*	
74. *Sio*, een Koe	a cow	*syo/so*	
75. *Jang*, een Schaep	a sheep	*yang*	
76. *Kay*, een Hond	a dog	*kahi/kae*	
77. *Sodse*, een Leeuw	a lion	*sǎjǎe/saja*	
78. *Jacktey*, een Kam-eel	a camel	*yaktae*	
79. *Toot**, een Varken	a pig	*tot/twaeji*	
80. *Tiarck*, een Hoen	a chicken	*tǎlk/ta[l]k*	
81. *Koely**, een Haen	a cock	?	
82. *Kookiri*, een Oly-phant	an elephant	*k'okkiri*	
83. *Kooy**, een Kat	a cat	*koe/koyangi*	
84. *t'Swy*, een Rot	a rat	*chwi*	
85. *Pajam**, een Slang	a snake	*pǎyam/paem*	
86. *Tootshavi**, een Duivel	a devil	*toch'aebi/tokkaebi*	
87. *Poetsia*, een Afgod	an idol	*put'yŏ, put'ye/puch'ŏ*	Buddha
88. *Kuym, Goud*	gold	*kŭm*	
89. *Gun*, Zilver	silver	*ŭn*	
90. *Naep*, Tin	tin, pewter	*nap*	lead, solder
91. *Jen*, Loot	lead	*yŏn*	
92. *Zooy*, yzer	iron	*soe*	
93. *t'Sybi*, een Huis	a house	*chip (chibi)*	
94. *Nara*, Land	land, country		

(original text)	(English or numerals)	(corrections in) transcription)	(corrections in translation)
95. *Jangsyck*, Rys	rice	*yangsik*	provisions, victuals
96. *t'Saet**, een Pot	a pot	?	
97. *Saeram*, een Mensch	a human being	*sarăm/saram*	
98. *Kackxie**, een Vrouw	a woman	*kaksi*	
99. *Ater*, een Kind	a child	*adăl/adŭl*	son
100. *Aickie**, een Jongen	a boy	*aegi/agi*	baby
101. *Boejong*, Lynwaet	linen	*mumyŏng*	cotton cloth, cotton
102. *Pydaen*, Zyde	silk	*pidan*	
103. *Samson**, stoffen	cloth	*samsŭng*	hemp cloth
104. *Koo*, de Neus	the nose	*k'o*	
105. *Taigwor**, 't Hooft	the head	*taegal*	
106. *Jyp*, de Mond	the mouth	*ip*	
107. *Spaem**, de Wangen	the cheeks	*ppam/ppyam*	
108. *Doen*, de Oogen	the eyes	*nun*	
109. *Pael*, de Voeten	the feet	*pal*	
110. *Stock*, Brood	bread	*ttŏk*	rice-cake
111. *Soer*, Arack	arrack	*sul*	rice-wine
112. *Podo*, Druiven	grapes	*p'odo*	
113. *Caem*, Orangie Appel	orange	*kam*	persimmon
114. *Goetsio*, Peper	pepper	*huch'u*	
115. *Satang*, Zuiker	sugar	*sadang*	
116. *Jaeck*, Artzeny	medicine	*yak*	
117. *t'So*, Edik	vinegar	*ch'o*	
118. *Paemi*, de Nacht	the night	*pam (pami)*	
119. *Jangsey**, de Dag	the day	?	
120. *More*, Morgen	to-morrow		the day after tomorrow
121. *Oodsey*, Over-morgen	the day after to-morrow	*ŏje*	yesterday
122. *Pha*, Ajuin	onion	*p'a*	
123. *Mannel*, Look	garlic	*manăl/manŭl*	
124. *Nammer**, Groente	vegetables	*namul*	

(original text)	(English or numerals)	(corrections in) transcription)	(corrections in translation)
125. *Nammo*, Hout	wood	*namo/namu*	
126. *Jury*, Glass	glass	*yuri*	
127. *Jurymano*, Spiegel glas	plate-glass	*yuri, mano*	glass, agate

127. *Jurimano*, a precious stone, a word also used for 'glass' by them.

128. *Poel*, Vuur	fire	*pul*	

129. *Pangamksio** is the word they use for tobacco and this means 'a herb coming from the south,' since the seed of tobacco seems to have been brought to them from *Japan* where it was introduced by the Portuguese.

130. *Jangman*, Edelman	nobleman	*yangban*	
131. *t'Jangsio*, Overste	commander-in-chief	*changsu*	

Names of the Months

132. *Tiongwor*, January	January	*chyŏngwŏl/chŏngwŏl*	
133. *Jyewor*, February	February	*iwŏl*	
134. *Samwor*, Maert	March	*samwŏl*	
135. *Soowor*, April	April	*săwŏl/sawŏl*	
136. *Ovoor*, Mey	May	*owŏl*	
137. *Joevoor**, Juny	June	*yuwol*	
138. *t'Syrvoor*, July	July	*ch'irwŏl*	
139. *Parvoor*, Augustus	August	*p'arwŏl*	
140. *Koevoor*, September	September	*kuwŏl*	
141. *Sievoor*, October	October	*siwŏl*	
142. *Tonsyter*, November	November	*tongjittăl/tongjittal*	
143. *Sutter* December	December	*sŏttăl, sŏttal*	

(8) In the Chŏlla dialect we find *yadal* and, especially in Chŏlla Namdo, *yadap.*[99]

(10) *yal* instead of *yŏl* is—according to Chŏng & Kim, *Chosŏn koŏ pang'ŏn sajŏn*—Hamgyŏng-do dialect.

(11-20) In all these instances the Korean and Sino-Korean readings of the numbers are combined, e.g. *Jeroptchil* (17) = *nilgop* 닐곱 *ch'il* 七. In the case of *hăn il, tu i* (not: *tul i*), *yŏdŏl[p] p'al* and *yŏl sip* the meanings of the compounds may refer to the radicals 1, 7, 12 and 24 (一, 二, 八, 十).

23 In Chŏlla Namdo: *maun, mahun*; a pronunciation like *mahăn* is very plausible.

29 It is interesting to note that Eibokken does not give the pure Korean words for 100 and 1000 (cf. 38): *on* and *chŭmŭn*.

38-46 Eibokken's *oock* (*ŏk* 億) should have been *man* 萬. Probably he forgot the word *man* or the correct meaning of *ŏk*. He probably had not had much to do with such large numbers of anything! Nowadays *ŏk* is 100 million, but formerly it stood for 100.000 (十萬爲億).

(52, 54, 55) We may assume that either Witsen or the printers got the numbers mixed up.

(56) *Jyoock* (*chyo/cho* 兆 or does Eibokken mean 十億?) is nowadays a trillion, but formerly it stood for one million (十億爲兆).

(57) Ikuta (*Chōsen yūshū-ki*, p. 154) obviously assumes a typographical error (*n* = *u*) here and identifies *pontchaa* (*poutchaa*?) with *poetsia* (87), but then God and idol would be the same. . . . *Ponjon* 本尊 (*satyadevatā*), 'the most honoured of all Buddhas', 'the chief object of worship in a group', seems more probable here. Phonetically *ponsă/ ponsa* 本師 (the original Master or Teacher, i.e. Sākyamuni) seems closer to *pontchaa*, but this term was (and is) hardly used in Korea.

(58) *mol* is Chŏlla dialect.

(59) Inexplicable. *Moolhoot* could hardly be a typographical error for *moltăl/maltŭl*!

(61) In Chŏlla Namdo dialect also: *hanŏl* and *hanul*.

---

[99]Much of my information concerning the Chŏlla and other dialects I owe to Chŏng T'aejin & Kim Pyŏngje, *Chosŏn koŏ pang'ŏn sajŏn*.

(72) *koegi* is Chŏlla dialect.

(73) *Moet koikie* (*mutkogi*) was a common term in the Yi period, meaning 'meat of land animals (*mut-chimsŭng*).'[101]

(79) Modern *twaeji* is probably the result of regressive synharmony: *tot* > *todi* > *toji* > *toeji* > *twaeji* (spelled *toaeji*).[102]

(81) Has the curious word *Koely* been inspired by *kugu*, 'cluck! cluck!', also used when calling chickens to feed them?[103]

(83) Actually *koe* is the word for 'cat' used in Hwanghae-do and Ch'ungch'ŏng Namdo; in Chŏlla Namdo (as in Seoul) a cat is called *koengi*.

(85) *păyam* in Middle Korean.

(86) *toch'aebi* is found in the dialects of Chŏlla and Cheju-do.

(96) Inexplicable.

(98) In Middle Korean *kaksi* was also used in the sense of 'woman', nowadays it only means 'doll' or 'bride.'

(100) *aegi* is a variant of, and Chŏlla Namdo dialect for *agi*. The reading *aegi* is, of course, also due to regressive synharmony.[104]

(103) *samsŭng* 三升 is a kind of cotton cloth, according to Gale (*A Korean-English Dictionary*, p. 507) imported from Mongolia; *samsŭngp'o* 三升布 = *sŏksaebe*, 'coarse hemp cloth.'

(105) In Middle Korean *tăegori* has the meaning of *mŏrit'ong*, 'the bulk of one's head.' Cf. Yu Ch'angdon, *Yi-jo ŏ-sajŏn*, p. 188. In the modern language *tăegari* (*taegal*) is a vulgar word for 'head.'

(107) *ppam* is Middle Korean and still used in the dialects of Chŏllado, Kyŏngsang Namdo and Hamgyŏng Namdo.

(119) *Jangsey* is inexplicable. In contrast to *pam* one would have expected *nat* (day, daytime) here. The *yang* is probably 陽 as in *t'aevang* 太陽ㅏ (sun).

(124) In Cheju dialect: *nămăl*.

(129) The correct reading is *nammanch'o*. Hamel writes *Nampancoij*.[105]

---

[101]Cf. Nam Kwang'u, *Koŏ sajŏn*, p. 223.

[102]Cf. Vos, "Historical Survey of Korean Language Studies," p. 20.

[103]Hypothesis of Mr. Kim Ilgŭn 金一根 (Seoul).

[104]Cf. Vos, *loc. cit.*

[105]*CA*, p. 223; *HV*, p. 49; *RN*, p. 341.

(137, 141) From his use of *yuwŏl* and *siwŏl* (instead of *yug'wŏl* and and *sib'wŏl*) we may deduce that Eibokken remembered certain peculiarities of the Korean Language very well!

*   *   *   *

From this vocabulary we may draw the following conclusions:

a. It is evident that Master Eibokken lived for many years (1656-1666) in Chŏlla Namdo (cf. nrs. 8, 58, 72, 86).

b. Several words may be identified as belonging to Middle Korean[106] (cf. nrs. 73, 79, 85, 107).

c. Eibokken must have been able to read, and probably also to write, *han'gŭl*. From the fact that a word like *ttae* 때 (time) was written as 째 around 1590, as 때 in 1617 and 1632, and afterwards again as 째 [107], it becomes clear that the consonant clusters ᄠ and ᄯ were pronounced in the same way—i.e. as *tt*—in the 16th and 17th centuries.[108] Since Eibokken spells *ppam* (107) and *ttŏk* (110) as *spaem* and *stock*, he must have known the old spelling of these words. Other evidence of his ability to read (and write?) the Korean alphabet is furnished by his renderings of 희 as *hay* (62), 쇼 as *sio* (74), 듕 as *tiarck* (80), 쉬 as *zooy* (92), and 애기 as *aickie*.

d. That he had no notes at his disposal, but quoted from memory becomes clear from such strange items as *moolhoot* (59), *koely* (81), *yangsey* (119) as well as from his wrong translations of *more* (120) and *oodsey* (121).

It is remarkable and regrettable that Eibokken's early contributions to Korean studies, and especially his pioneer vocabulary, have not attracted more attention in the scholarly world, but this is probably due to the fact that Witsen's work appeared only in Dutch.

---

[106]For a definition of Middle Korean (1446-1824) *vide* Seung-bog Cho, *A phonological Study of Korean*, p. 5.

[107]Cf. Nam Kwang'u, *op. cit.*, p. 147.

[108]See also Cho, *op. cit.*, pp. 194-204, and Kim Hyŏnggyu, [*Chŭngbo*] *Kug'ŏ-sa yŏn'gu*, pp. 65-70.

GENERAL REFERENCE

The Dutch Come to Korea, Gari Ledyard, R.A.S. Korea Branch Monograph Series no. 3 (1971)

A Forbidden Land: Voyages to the Corea, Ernest Oppert, New York G.P. Putnam's Sons (1880)

History of Corea, Rev. J. Ross (1880)

Histoire de l'Eglise de Corée, Ch. Dallet (1874)

Corea, Without and Within, William Eliot Griffis (1885)

Corea, the Hermit Kingdom, William Eliot Griffis (1905)

Noord en Oost Tartarije, Nicolaes Witsen, second edition, Amsterdam (1705)

From the Study of Nicolaes Witsen (1641-1717). His life with books and manuscripts, Marion Peters, LIAS, Vol. 21, 1994

VOC, A bibliography of publications relating to the Dutch East India Company (1620-1800), Peter van der Krogt, Utrecht, 1991

Master Eibokken on Korea and the Korean Language: Supplementary Remarks to Hamel's Narrative, Frits Vos, Transactions, R.A.S. Korea Branch, 1975

Some Background Notes on the Dutch in Korea in the 17th Century Johannes Huber, Transactions, R.A.S. Korea Branch, 1991